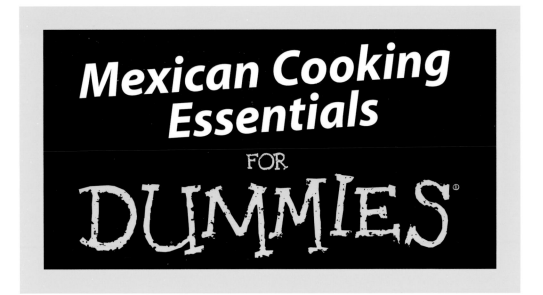

Mexican Cooking
Essentials
FOR
DUMMIES®

Susan Feniger & Mary Sue Milliken

with Helene Siegel

COURAGE
BOOKS

AN IMPRINT OF RUNNING PRESS
PHILADELPHIA · LONDON

Library of Congress Cataloging-in-Publication Number 2002100364

ISBN 0-7624-1399-9

Jacket and interior designed by Matthew Goodman
Edited by Michael Washburn
Typography: Cheltenham, Univers, Cascade Script, Myriad

Photo Credits:

© William B. Folsom, Photography, Inc.: front cover and spot photos

© Corbis: back cover

Photos courtesy of H. Armstrong Roberts:
© Hersel Abernathy: pp. 53, 112
© Jim Graham: pp. 29, 35, 54, 84, 100
© Ed Masterson: p. 36
© John Neubauer: p. 3
© Kenneth Rice: pp. 8, 12

This book may be ordered by mail from the publisher. Please include $2.50 for postage and handling.
But try your bookstore first!

Published by Courage Books, an imprint of
Running Press Book Publishers
125 South Twenty-second Street
Philadelphia, Pennsylvania 19103-4399

Visit us on the web!
www.runningpress.com

Icons used in this book

 These are technique tips or shortcuts for reducing kitchen stress. They usually show an easy, fast way to do something.

 This icon indicates ways to avoid common pitfalls and problems. Remember, you've been warned!

 A variation following a recipe gives instructions for different ways to tweak and turn the preceding recipe to give it another twist of flavor. Variations can help you make a dish even though you are missing an ingredient, and they can also help you develop a more flexible way of viewing recipes in general.

 Even business partners can disagree sometimes. This icon flags Mary Sue's personal pet peeves, ideas, and suggestions.

 When you see this icon, expect some words from Susan—she's the short one who can't stop cooking and talking, in her own words.

Table of Contents

Chapter 1

• • • • • • • • • •

Understanding Mexican Cooking

In This Chapter

• • • • • • • • • • • • • •

▶ Debunking common Mexican food myths
  ▶ Getting a taste for Mexican cooking

• • • • • • • • • • • • • •

Forget about those cheesy restaurant combination platters of yesterday, with their heaping portions of rice, beans, and fried foods. Our style of Mexican cooking is much lighter than that, and it can be as hot and spicy as you like. Big flavors, inexpensive ingredients, ease of preparation, and casual presentation are what our kind of Mexican cooking is all about.

The recipes in this book include a range of dishes—a whole fish marinated in citrus juices and spice and tossed on the grill, succulent pork and chile tamales, bracing raw and cooked fish cocktails, big soups and stews brimming with chunks of fresh vegetables and lime juice, and enough interesting new salads to please the vegetarians and light eaters in the house. Here are a few myths you can toss aside once you start cooking with us.

Myth #1: Mexican food is too spicy

To think of Mexican food as merely hot and spicy is to oversimplify a much more complicated set of sensations. The great traditional foods of Mexico, like moles and posoles, are a complex blend of savory and earthy flavors, with chopped condiments and spicy salsas generally served on the side to use as a seasoning and for textural contrast.

For some reason, perhaps because it was a hot concept that could be easily communicated, spiciness became the defining characteristic of all things Mexican in the United States. It just ain't so.

Myth #2: Mexican food is too heavy

Old-fashioned Mexican-American restaurant food is heavy. Real Mexican food and the modern updates we favor feature lots of fresh fruits and vegetables, herb garnishes, fresh chopped salsas, rice, beans, tortillas, and a small serving of meat or chicken. Modern Mexican cuisine is light and healthful, with a large dose of flavor.

All that sour cream and melted cheese associated with Mexican food is actually an American restaurant innovation. Typical corn and tortilla snacks, such as enchiladas, tacos, and quesadillas, are meant to be delicate, nutrient-dense morsels, not the leaden doorstops they can be in the United States. Think back to the big, heavy platters of meatballs and spaghetti of the 1950s that have become the refined vegetable pastas of today and you can see the direction Mexican food is taking.

Myth #3: Mexican food is hard to cook

It's ironic that such a rustic, family style of cooking is intimidating to American home cooks. For many, it remains a food to go out to restaurants for, rather than something to cook themselves.

Getting Started with Mexican Cooking

Start small, with familiar, accessible foods like tacos or marinated and grilled meats with salsas. Save the 28-ingredient mole and the more technique-intensive tamales for some time down the road when you have a weekend to tool around the kitchen and linger over a pot of stew.

Get to know one or two chiles well—serranos and poblanos are a good place to start. After you feel comfortable with your "starter chiles," then branch out to other, more exotic chiles. The techniques for roasting, peeling, and seeding are the same no matter what kind of chile you cook with.

If you're a weekend cook, increase your popularity by entertaining Mexican-style. You can't go wrong with chips, salsas, guacamole, two or three kinds of tacos, and a pitcher full of margaritas in the house.

Be daring: Taste that baby goat taco at the ethnic food stand, mix up a drink with dried hibiscus flowers, and surprise your friends with homemade tamales or salsas during the holidays. Mexican food is all about expanding your horizons and breaking out of familiar, dull food habits. Remember that before you started cooking pasta every night of the week, Italian food was new and foreign.

Chapter 2

· · · · · · · · · ·

Ingredients, Tools, and Techniques

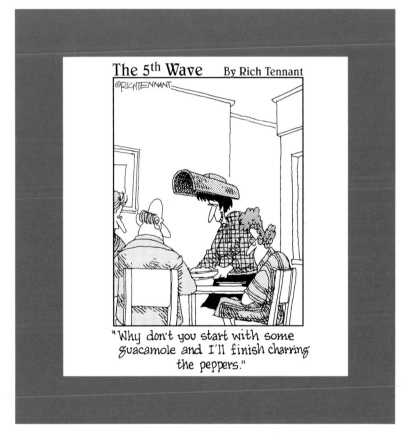

The 5th Wave By Rich Tennant

"Why don't you start with some guacamole and I'll finish charring the peppers."

In This Chapter

· · · · · · · · · · · · · ·

▸ Stocking the pantry for everyday cooking

▸ Demestifying the almighty chile

▸ Selecting equipment for your kitchen

▸ Discovering the techniques used in Mexican cooking

· · · · · · · · · · · · · · · · ·

Fruits and Vegetables

Tropical fruits like mango, pineapple, guava, and watermelon—beautifully sliced and seasoned—are sold on the street as snacks and pureed into mouthwatering drinks at juice stands all over Mexico.

And vegetables are not some sad little afterthoughts that appear alongside a big serving of meat. They're sliced, diced, and pureed into sauces, stews, and garnishes that make any vegetarian smile. Along with fruits, vegetables such as cucumbers and jícama are also eaten as snacks throughout the day.

Avocado

Pebbly-skinned greenish brown Hass (rhymes with pass) avocados are our first choice for Mexican cooking. Their rich, nutty flesh strikes the perfect balance with fiery Mexican foods, and this avocado is irreplaceable for guacamole, salads, sandwiches, tacos, and soups.

Our second favorite type, if you can't find high-quality Hass avocados, is the leaner, smooth-skinned Fuerte. Its flesh is more watery and the seed bigger than the Hass.

When shopping for avocados, remember that this is one fruit that shouldn't be judged by its cover. The condition of the skin is not necessarily an indication of what lies within. Sometimes scaly, blemished skin can cover the most luxurious flesh.

For judging ripeness, we rely on the squeeze test. If the flesh has a little give when you press it with a finger, you should plan on using the avocado within a day. However, if it puts up no resistance and squishes beneath your thumb, you should put it back. The flesh inside is probably already turning brown and losing its flavor.

Rock hard fruit takes about a week to ripen. To ripen avocados, store them in a sealed brown bag on the counter for about a week. An apple placed in the bag speeds up the process.

To remove the pit from an avocado and extract the meat, just follow these steps:

1. Cut the avocado in half lengthwise and pull the halves apart.

2. Place the half with the pit in it on a counter and hit the pit with the sharp edge of a heavy knife until it plunges in.

3. Twist the blade to remove the pit.

4. Scoop out the meat with a spoon.

After you cut an avocado, the flesh spoils quickly. To slow down the aging process, you can sprinkle the flesh with lemon or lime juice or cover the avocado skin-tight with plastic wrap and store the fruit in the fridge.

Banana leaves

Large, green banana leaves are available all year-round in the freezer section of Latin American markets. They're popular in the southern and Gulf coast states for wrapping fish, tamales, pork, and chicken. In addition to keeping foods moist, these fragrant green leaves impart a delicious fruity flavor of their own. They can also be used to line and cover pans for roasting meats.

To soften banana leaves for folding, use a knife to trim out and discard the tough stalk in the center. Then pass the leaf over a low gas or electric burner less than a minute until it becomes pliable. Because the leaves are huge, trim them into 9-inch squares for wrapping. Unused leaves can be tightly wrapped and stored in the freezer for several months.

Cactus paddles

The type of cactus most often eaten in Mexico is the prickly pear, the one traditionally pictured in movies about the Old West. Cooks in Mexico simply go into their front or backyards and cut off the tender, young paddles, no larger than about 6 by 8 inches, of the cactus as needed, just as you might harvest an herb or vegetable.

Look for cactus paddles, or *nopales* (noh-PAHl-es), also from the prickly pear, at farmers markets or ethnic grocers. They're usually sold already cleaned (with their needles removed), in plastic bags. The best, freshest paddles are bright green and firm and reverberate when flicked with a finger.

You may have to buy your cactus paddles au naturel and clean them yourself. The best way to remove the needles is to shave across the paddle with a sharp paring knife. Store the cleaned paddles in plastic bags in the vegetable bin of the refrigerator.

Boiling, which some cookbooks recommend, enhances their okra-like quality, but we don't recommend it. If you wish to try it anyway, simply bring a large pot of salted water to a boil and blanch the paddles as you would any green vegetable to soften slightly, about 3 minutes.

Chayote

This pale green, pear-shaped squash was one of the principal foods of the Aztec and Mayan people of Central America. We admire the bland little vegetable for its versatility, ease of preparation, and low cost. Also known as the *mirliton* in Louisiana, the chayote mixes the mild taste of zucchini with the firmer texture of a kohlrabi. Chayote is low in calories and an excellent source of potassium.

You can use chayote in any recipe calling for a summer squash such as zucchini, and everything, including the large seed in the center, is edible. You can also eat it raw in salads. Look for chayote in Latin and Asian markets year-round. Choose small, unblemished squashes and store them in the vegetable bin of the refrigerator as long as a month.

Corn husks

Dried corn husks are sold in packages at the supermarket year-round. They are the traditional wrapper for tamales, but you can use them to wrap other foods for steaming or grilling: Achiote-marinated fish strips for the steamer or slices of lime-marinated pork loin for the grill are two mouthwatering examples. Corn husks protect tender foods as they cook, while infusing them with corn essence.

One package of husks is usually enough to wrap about 1 dozen tamales. Store dry husks in an airtight package in the pantry as long as a year.

Dried husks should always be soaked in hot water before using—you'll need to soak them for at least 2 hours. Choose the largest pieces for wrapping and shred thin strings from the edges for tying tamale packages closed.

Jícama

Jícama is one root vegetable it pays to know. This plain, round, brown-skinned root yields crisp, white flesh that's terrific for adding sparkle to salads and raw vegetable platters.

Like water chestnuts in Chinese cooking, jícama is primarily a texture food. In Mexico, jícama is cut into sticks, sprinkled with salt, cayenne, and lime juice, and sold on the street as a snack. Because its flavor is rather bland (it's mildly sweet like a water chestnut), it always needs at least some salt and lemon or lime to perk it up.

Look for jícama in the produce section of the supermarket. Always remove the fibrous brown skin with a knife and, once cut, cover the flesh with plastic wrap to avoid drying. You can store jícama in the vegetable bin of the refrigerator for a few days.

Lime

Mexican cooks use the yellow-skinned key lime, or limón as it is called there, and the taste is sweeter than the limes typically eaten elsewhere. The lime is used in Mexico for marinating fish and chicken, perking up salsas, garnishing soups, and balancing margaritas, among other uses.

If you can't find key limes in your local supermarket, you can create a similar taste at home. Just mix half lemon juice and half lime juice any time a recipe calls for lime juice to get closer to the true Mexican flavor.

In the United States, the green Persian lime is the most widely available lime. Persian limes can be disappointingly hard, juiceless, *and* expensive to boot. Choose them wisely: Look for small, soft, thin-skinned fruit, with a yellowish tint in the supermarket or farmers market.

Store limes in a bowl or basket on the countertop. Don't put them in the refrigerator—they go bad faster in there!

We prefer to juice limes by hand. Roll them on the counter first, bearing down to break up the juice sacs. Then cut the lime in half across its width and, holding a half in one hand, plunge the tines of a fork into the pulp. Twist the fork to loosen the juice and pour into a bowl.

If juicing a quantity of limes in advance, you can store the juice in a sealed jar in the refrigerator up to 2 days. Or, if your quantity is really large, transfer the juice to freezer bags and freeze it. For smaller portions, freeze the juice in ice cube trays. You never want to be caught without lime juice.

For an extra-concentrated pop of lime flavor in rich stews and soups, try using diced pulp rather than the juice and zest. Using a serrated blade, first remove all of the zest and the white pith beneath it. Then dice the pulp and add it toward the end of your recipe's cooking time.

It can be tempting in the rush to get the meal on the table to substitute bottled lime or lemon juice for fresh citrus juice, but don't! There is such a difference in taste between that chemical cocktail sold in bottles and the real thing. For neat little lime wedges, as they are cut in Mexico, first trim off the ends of the lime with a sharp paring knife. Then cut the lime in half crosswise. Laying each half on the counter, cut side down, cut in half and half again.

Plantains

These large, thick, cooking bananas are a staple food in the Caribbean, where they're fried, mashed, boiled, simmered, pureed, and baked into soups, stews, breads, and side dishes. Though classified as a fruit, like the banana, plantains are used more as a starchy root vegetable like a yam by Caribbean cooks, including those of Mexico's Yucatán peninsula.

The trick to handling plantains is knowing their stages of ripeness. Their color ranges from green when picked to black when thoroughly ripe, and though you can cook them at every stage, they only turn sweet when their skin has entirely blackened, and their starch has turned to sugar. A cooked green plantain more closely resembles a potato than a banana.

If you plan to enjoy them sweet, purchase plantains that are yellow to black rather than entirely green because green fruit may be difficult to ripen. To speed up the ripening process, store fruit wrapped in newspapers or a brown paper bag out of sunlight, and add an apple if you wish to speed up the ripening process.

Tomatillos

These small, pale green fruits are the key to most green salsas. Though they resemble green tomatoes when out of the husk, tomatillos are acidic, pale-green members of the Cape Gooseberry family, and bear no relation to tomatoes.

Look for tomatillos that are small, not rock hard, and still in the husk in the supermarket produce section. Store tomatillos, in the husk, in the vegetable bin of the refrigerator. When you are ready to use them, just pull off the papery husks with your fingers and rinse off the fruit's naturally sticky coating with cold water.

Our favorite way to eat tomatillos is raw or very briefly cooked in order to retain their crunch and spunky bright flavor. Try them chopped in place of the tomatoes in a Fresh Salsa or diced and marinated in some lime juice and olive oil and spooned over raw oysters.

Chiles 101

Though chile peppers are enjoyed all over the world, no other country matches Mexico's passion for peppers. Mexican farmers grow over 140 varieties, and Mexican cooks are legendary for their skilled appreciation of every facet (not just the heat) of this complex vegetable that's technically a fruit.

From snappy, sparkly jalapeños to smoky chipotles and earthy poblanos, chiles are a light, healthful way to bring a wide range of strong, new flavors to your cooking. Just start with a little at a time, find out what you like, and don't let all the macho hype about the heat deter you.

If you're totally new to chiles and you're the type who likes to dip a toe in the water before diving in, start out gently. Try adding a dried pepper or two to a pot of your favorite soup or stew and let it steep until it plumps up. Then remove the chile before serving. The flavor of the chile will infuse the broth, but no one will be scorched by a mouthful of heat.

Shopping for chiles

A general rule for predicting the flavor and heat of a chile is the smaller the chile, the hotter the heat. Red indicates a ripe, and probably sweeter, chile than green. Cutting off and tasting a tiny piece of a slice of fresh chile is really the best way to predict its heat and flavor when cooked.

When purchasing fresh chiles, look for bright, smooth, shiny skin and buy about a week's supply. Store the chiles in the vegetable bin of the refrigerator and rinse them before using. Dried chiles should be fragrant and flexible enough to bend without breaking. Look for unbroken chiles that are not too dusty. (Because chiles are dried outdoors, they can become dirty and dusty and need to be wiped off before cooking.) Store dried chiles in airtight bags in the freezer and let them soften a minute or two at room temperature before using.

Handling fresh chiles

After chopping or otherwise handling chiles, you want to be mindful of the other surfaces that have come in contact with cut chiles. The hot oils from the cut chiles will spread like, you guessed it, wildfire.

Immediately after handling chiles, wash off your cutting boards, knives, and hands with hot, soapy water. Be careful not to touch your face or eyes before hand washing because chile oil in the eye is not fun.

Some cooks like to wear gloves when handling chiles, and some cooks coat their hands with a layer of cooking oil to protect them. Just wash with soap and water to remove the oil.

Plumping up dried chiles

Dried chiles are often rehydrated by taking a long soak in hot water or stock before joining the dish. Softening a not-too-hard chile takes about 20 minutes. Read the recipe all the way through before tossing out the soaking liquid because this chile-infused liquid is often called for later in the recipe.

Dried chiles have a whole other texture and taste, and should not be used as a substitute for fresh chiles. Just like fresh chiles, they can be toasted to improve flavor and seeds can be removed to reduce heat.

In our cooking, we rely on the nine types of chiles described in this section.

Ancho

Anchos are the dried version of our favorite green pepper, the poblano. This wrinkled red-brown, wide-shouldered chile has a mellow, sweet flavor, similar to a bell pepper, with just a touch of heat. We like to add it, julienned, to sauces for its chewy texture or pureed at the beginning of a sauce to add body and pure pepper flavor.

Chile de arbol

Arbols, also known as dried red chiles, are the papery thin, long, dried chiles sold by the bag in the supermarket. Used extensively in Chinese and Mexican cooking (they put the pow in Kung Pau chicken), these inexpensive little peppers pack a powerful punch of heat, especially after they're chopped and cooked. To tame their heat, you can add them whole to stews and soups and remove them before serving.

Chile negro or dried pasilla

This long, narrow, dark brown chile is a dried chilaca chile. Similar in flavor to the more popular ancho, pasillas are often used in combination with other dried chiles in traditional moles. Look for them via mail order or in ethnic markets.

Chipotle

Chipotles, or dried, smoked, red jalapeños, are one of those life-changing ingredients. Once we tasted chipotle salsa, on our first tasting expedition to Mexico back in 1984, we never looked back. We've been using these wrinkled, reddish-brown chiles to add a mysterious, smoky, sweet flavor to everything from salad dressings to grilled chicken and salsas ever since.

If you can't find dried chipotles at the market, try ordering them mail order. Though usable as a substitute, canned chipotles en adobo (dried chiles packed in a sweet, sour, spicy sauce) are quite different. They're actually hotter and their texture is softer. If you use chipotles en adobo, wipe them off to remove excess sauce and reduce by half the quantity called for in the recipe.

Habañero

This is one little pepper that lives up to its reputation. It's pure heat. Along with the Scotch Bonnet, the habañero is considered the world's hottest chile. These small, lantern-shaped (usually) peppers are most often used in the Yucatán. You can shop for them at Latin and farmers markets where their color can range from dark green to orange and even red. We prefer the taste of fresh rather than dried habañeros and recommend substituting a larger quantity of serranos (seeds and all) in a pinch.

Jalapeño, red and green

The jalapeño, America's favorite chile pepper, is a thick-fleshed, small (about 3-inch long), bright green or red pepper. With its sweet, fresh, garden flavor and medium heat, this versatile pepper is great for garnishing just about anything.

In Mexico, we've even seen jalapeños eaten as an accompaniment to rich stews and tacos. In fact, at the Border Grill staff meals, a bowl of fresh jalapeños is always nearby. They're easy to find at the market, but you can substitute serranos if you prefer. Canned jalapeños are not a good substitute for fresh peppers because their taste and texture are quite different.

Morita

These small, brown, dried chiles look like thin chipotles but are less smoky with a spicier taste. They are a variety of dried, smoked jalapeño. Use fewer moritas to replace chipotles in a recipe.

Poblano

These dark green, medium-sized, thick-fleshed chiles are our favorite fresh green peppers for cooking. We feature them in soups, sauces, and chilis, and they are always our first choice for stuffing because of their wide shoulders, thick skin, and smoldering flesh. They are superb as *rajas* (roasted pepper strips) because of their meatiness.

Sometimes mislabeled pasilla in the West, look for smooth-skinned poblano chiles with nice wide shoulders for stuffing. Less spicy, skinnier Anaheims can be substituted for stuffing, but poblanos should be easy to find in a well-stocked supermarket.

Serrano

Small, thin serranos are similar to jalapeños but pack a little more punch. We mostly use the green variety (the reds are a bit sweeter) in salsas and as a raw garnish in salads and soups. They're easy to find at the supermarket, and you can use them interchangeably with jalapeños.

Herbs

If the variety of herbs on the market makes you feel insecure, you can relax. The Mexican kitchen uses the same three herbs over and over again: cilantro, oregano (fresh and dried), and epazote. If you start cooking Mexican often, you may want to buy a few of these easy-to-grow plants for the garden and save last-minute shopping trips.

Cilantro

If the thought of a cilantro leaf passing your lips still makes you quiver after a few tastes, please don't give up on Mexican food. Simply replace it with flat leaf parsley or an herb that you love and, if anybody asks, tell them two highly trained chefs gave you permission.

Cilantro, also known as Chinese parsley or fresh coriander, was brought to Mexico by the Spanish. It is primarily used fresh in salsas and as a garnish, but is also cooked into green moles, sauces, and stews. Look for it in the supermarket produce section and store the bunch, loosely covered with a plastic bag, stems down, in a glass of water in the refrigerator.

If the roots are still attached, leave them on. Because cilantro is so delicate, it's best not to chop it in advance. Likewise, don't stress about removing the thin stems; they're entirely edible. Dried cilantro should never be used to replace fresh. This is one herb that doesn't dry well.

Epazote

Stronger-tasting than most herbs, epazote grows like the weed that it is all over North America. It's difficult to find in the supermarket (though you're liable to find it in the weeds growing alongside the highway in Los Angeles), but you can easily grow it from seed in the garden or a pot. We've tried the dried variety and do not recommend it because it's virtually flavorless. The flavor of fresh epazote is so dominant that it should be used alone, not in combination with other herbs, when flavoring a dish. In Mexico, it's often used to complement mushrooms, black beans, squash, and even quesadillas. When cooking with epazote, always trim off the tough stem.

Oregano

Oregano, familiar from Italian-American cooking, is the most popular herb in the Mexican kitchen. Thirteen varieties of this small, soft, green-leafed plant grow in Mexico. Look for it in the supermarket produce section and always remove the leaves from the tough stems.

Mexican cooks also use dried oregano. You can purchase cellophane bags of Mexican dried oregano, containing larger pieces of leaves and stems, and crumble the large pieces by hand before adding or just use common dried oregano. We sometimes add a smoky edge by toasting the dried herb first in a dry skillet over low heat.

The Spice Shelf

The Mexican spice shelf is reassuringly short: cumin for savor and cinnamon for sweetness. The magic lies in how these spices are combined with chiles, salt, pepper, assorted seeds, and other flavorings to make this simple soul-satisfying cuisine.

Cumin

We recommend using it liberally in your Mexican cooking, combined with cinnamon, nutmeg, cayenne, and arbol chiles for a sweet spicy kick, or combined with onion, garlic, ground ancho, paprika, and cayenne for a full, earthy, chile flavor.

Use it ground, if you want its flavor to pervade the dish, and always develop the flavor by cooking it first in fat. Use about 1 teaspoon of whatever fat is in the dish to each teaspoon of spice. If it's just dropped into a bubbling soup or stew, the flavor never goes as deep. Use cumin seeds whole when you're looking for an assertive pop of flavor when you take a bite.

As with all dried spices, you can purchase cumin in small enough quantities to last on your shelf no longer than six months. Store out of sunlight and check expiration dates in the store before purchasing. You're likely to find fresher cumin in an Indian or Mexican market where cooks purchase it a lot.

Cinnamon

Cinnamon, known as *canela* in Spanish, is used in the Mexican kitchen to flavor both savories and sweets. The thin, papery, brown bark known as Mexican cinnamon has a rougher edge and is less expensive than the tightly wound variety commonly found in the supermarket. Look for the Mexican variety (actually from Sri Lanka), packed in hanging cellophane bags, in the ethnic section of the market. Use the bark to infuse drinks, stews, moles, and sauces and then discard it. Ground cinnamon can always be used in its place.

Store cinnamon in airtight containers away from the sun and replenish after about six months because the bark dries out.

Nuts, Seeds, and Seasoning Pastes

Nuts and seeds are much more than a snack food or dessert ingredient in the Mexican kitchen. Since pre-Columbian times, peanuts, pecans, and pumpkin seeds have been used to thicken sauces and moles. And the Spanish influence can be seen in the use of almonds and walnuts in rich ground-nut sauces and stuffings. Nut- and seed-based sauces come under the general heading of pipians, of which Green Pumpkin Seeds Mole is one.

Annatto seed and achiote paste

These tiny, rock hard, brick red seeds from the South American annatto tree give Mexican food its characteristic orange tint.

The seeds alone have a slightly musky flavor but when ground and combined with garlic, oregano, cumin, cinnamon, pepper, and cloves they make fragrant achiote paste, a seasoning mixture popular in the Yucatán for marinades and sauces.

Annatto seed, available in ethnic markets and by mail order, is used by American food producers to add an orange tint to butter and cheddar cheese. You can use the seeds to flavor an oil by simply heating them in the oil and then straining out the seeds, or you can grind them in a coffee or spice grinder and use them to color masa for tamales. Annatto or achiote should always be cooked in fat to remove any chalkiness.

Achiote paste, sold in bricks in Mexican markets, is an easy-to-use spice rub for fish and meats. When the paste is thinned with vinegar or citrus juices, the spices develop a wonderful tropical fruitiness. Achiote paste can be kept, well wrapped, in the refrigerator for a long time.

Be sure to wash off any utensils or cutting boards that come into contact with annatto or achiote right away. There's a reason this is an industrial-strength dye. A little goes a long way.

Tamarind seeds and paste

Tamarind is a leathery, dried brown seed pod that produces a deliciously sticky, sweet-sour paste when cooked. One of the key ingredients in Worcestershire sauce, it is popular in Indian, Mexican, Indonesian, and Thai cuisines as a tart balance to fatty foods. It is available in brick as well as pod form in ethnic markets.

To reconstitute dried tamarind pods, first remove the hard outer pods by hand and discard the pods. Place the fruit in a pan, generously cover with water, and cook at a boil about 15 minutes, until soft. Strain before using. The finished paste should be the consistency of ketchup.

Bricks of tamarind pulp should be soaked in hot water to soften about 30 minutes and then pressed through a strainer to separate any solids from the thick puree. A good substitute for tamarind paste is pureed, dried apricots, enhanced with some lemon juice.

Coconut

The best ones feel heavy in your hand and sound full of liquid when shaken. If the eyes are soft and the coconut smells spoiled when you sniff it, chances are that it's rotten inside.

In some Latin markets, coconuts are sold already husked and wrapped to go in plastic. But if you can't get to a Latin market, here's how to get to that sweet, white meat: Poke a hole in two or three eyes with a screwdriver or ice pick and drain the liquid. Place the coconut on a baking tray in a 350° oven for about 10 minutes, and then remove it and crack it open with a hammer on the floor (to avoid damage to your expensive kitchen counters).

For delicious, large shards of coconut meat ready-to-go, shop for unsweetened, shaved (not shredded) coconut in health food markets. Store the coconut in plastic bags in the freezer.

Pepitas

Pumpkin seeds, or pepitas, are native to Mexico and show up in sauces, salads, moles, and, of course, snack foods. The seeds sold in Mexico, often with the thin, white husks still on, have much more flavor than those sold in the United States. The thin husks are edible.

We like to purchase the long, thin green seeds raw from bulk markets and season them with Chili Mix Powder and salt, spread them on a baking sheet, and roast them in the oven until crisp.

Like all seeds and nuts, pepitas should be stored in airtight containers in the freezer. They need not be defrosted before using.

Beans and Starches

These beans and starches are the simple and substantial backbones of every Mexican meal.

Beans

The two beans Americans most often associate with Mexican cooking are black beans and larger mottled pink pintos, but in Mexico, people enjoy a wider variety. Beans and rice are served at virtually every meal to ensure a daily dose of protein in diets that don't depend upon a large portion of meat.

Most important when shopping for beans is to purchase from a store that does a brisk business. There is such a thing as a bean that's gotten too old to ever cook up soft—and it's impossible to spot these little scoundrels before they're cooked.

If you don't have time for all the boiling dried beans require, you can always substitute a good canned bean. A good way to enhance the flavor of canned beans is to sauté a clove or two of garlic with a chopped onion in some oil until they are soft and nearly brown. Add this to the beans with their cooking liquid and warm through.

Tortillas

You can't eat Mexican food without tortillas. Deep yellow corn tortillas are our favorite, but white can be good too, depending on your preference. You can use corn tortillas for making chips, enchiladas, chilaquiles, and tostadas, to name a few dishes, and they'll keep a long time in their sealed package in the fridge.

Flour tortillas, with or without lard, are also available in various sizes and packs in the supermarket. You may want to stock these tortillas if you like making burritos and quesadillas. Also, search for uncooked tortilla dough in the supermarket freezer next to the cookie dough.

Masa harina

Masa harina is flour made from corn dough that has been dried and then ground into a powder. Quaker Oats sells it in the supermarket baking section. Ordinary yellow cornmeal for making cornbread is not a good substitute.

The Mexican Dairy

Authentic Mexican cheeses can be found in most supermarkets. With the three basic cooking cheeses—panela, añejo, and manchego—or their substitutes, you have all the cheeses you ever need to cook authentic quesadillas or queso fundido, or just add a bite of richness to salads, soups, and enchiladas. Remember, as a general culinary principle, just say no to orange cheese.

Añejo

Also known as Cotija (koh-TEE-jah), for the town where it was first made, añejo (ah-NYEH-hoh) is a dry, aged cow's milk cheese prized for its salty bite. Because it's not a good melter, it should always be combined with another cheese in cooked dishes, but for sprinkling over beans, soups, and salads it is perfect alone. Use it as you would grated Parmesan in your Italian cooking. Either Parmesan or Romano makes a good substitute.

Panela

Panela, a semi-soft white cow's milk cheese, has a delightfully fresh milky flavor. In the freshest panela, the curds are still visible, as well as the circular pattern imprinted from the basket in which the curds were set to drain. We like it diced, as a garnish for soup or posole, and in cubes in a salad because it holds its shape so well.

Contrary to its mozzarella-like appearance, panela is not a good melter and always needs to be teamed with a Jack-like cheese for quesadillas. We recommend dry curd farmer's cheese, dry cottage, or dry ricotta as substitutes.

Mexican manchego

This inexpensive semi-soft cheese should not be confused with Spanish manchego, a stronger aged eating cheese. Soft, mild Mexican manchego is the melter in the group. You can substitute Monterey Jack cheese for manchego.

Crema

Mexican crema, sold in jars in the refrigerator case of the supermarket, is a soured milk product similar to buttermilk and sour cream. This salty, white drizzling cream is thinner and less sour than sour cream and used most often as a garnish or dressing.

We're not big fans of commercial produced crema because of the additives. The best substitute is crème fraiche, but sour cream thinned with a bit of lime juice or buttermilk to the consistency of a creamy salad dressing will do in a pinch.

The cheese mix

We like to use a grated mixture of one part manchego, one part panela, and one part añejo rather than one cheese in our cooked dishes. The mix results in a more complex texture and flavor. Manchego lends its texture, añejo its salt, and panela its milkiness.

Of course, if you can't get your hands on all three, feel free to improvise with substitutes or use two rather than three types of cheese. The basic idea is that a variety of cheeses is always preferable to one in any melted cheese dish.

Olives

The most authentic olives for Mexican cooking are little green Manzanillas from Spain, with pits, not pimentos. They're sold in ethnic markets and the ethnic section of the supermarket.

Here's what we recommend for working on all four burners:

- ✔ Invest in a starter set of cookware that includes 14- and 10-inch skillets, a 3-quart saucepan, and a 10-quart stockpot. Purchasing pieces that may be too large for your present needs is better than buying small pans. Empty space in a skillet is less of a problem than overcrowding. A brisk sauté can become a slow steam in moments in a pan that's too small.

- ✔ Our favorite materials are heat conductors like copper, aluminum, and cast iron. Heavier pots and pans not only cook better but also last longer.

- ✔ Avoid fancy cookware with bottoms made of a different material from the body of the pan. Those sandwiched bottoms can separate and warp over time. Also avoid plastic handles because they'll melt and warp in the oven. If you can afford only one good knife, make it a large, 10-inch heavy chef's knife. Hold the knife in your hand and make sure that the grip is comfortable. The blade should be well-balanced with a full *tang*— the metal running the length of the knife from tip to handle.

To sharpen knives with a steel, hold the knife at a 30-degree angle and swipe the entire edge of the blade against the steel. Repeat about 10 times on each side for an even edge. After a knife has totally lost its edge, take it to a professional cutlery store to put the edge back on with a device known as a stone.

Blenders

We're always shocked to see blenders in remote villages in Mexico, but there is really nothing like them for all the grinding and pureeing involved in making Mexican beverages, sauces, moles, and stuffings. It's the only piece of electric equipment you'll ever need, and we would choose a blender any day over a food processor.

Although a processor has a bigger work bowl and more powerful motor, it whirs everything around so quickly that some pieces of food get pushed to the edges, never getting properly ground. But a blender, because of the tall shape of the container and blade design, processes foods up and down, resulting in an even grind every time.

Any inexpensive blender will do, but a blender with a heavier case and more powerful motor is always a better investment over the long haul because it will last longer.

Stovetop grills and griddles

Those circular cross-hatched grates that fit over a burner are great for heating tortillas on the stovetop, although a hot, dry skillet works just fine.

We also like heavy stovetop grill pans for getting a grilled effect indoors. And a low-edged pancake griddle is great for reaching right in and flipping freshly made tortillas.

Tortilla presses

Metal and wooden tortilla presses for pressing out dough are sold at Mexican markets and by mail order from cookware catalogs.

The cheaper the better—you shouldn't pay more than about $8 for one. Just look for a press that presses the dough evenly at all points. They pretty much explain themselves once you get one in your hands. (Press down with the lever to squash the dough.) In a pinch, we've pressed tortillas between sheets of plastic, with a good heavy dictionary—Spanish or English.

You can put your tortilla press to work by making flour tortillas or corn tortillas.

Bean mashers

We like the inexpensive, wiggly, wire, handheld variety—good for mashing refried beans and potatoes but leaving a few lumps of authenticity.

Steamers

The little perforated baskets that fit in a saucepan for steaming vegetables are great for Mexican cooking. You can improvise a larger steamer for tamales by fitting a colander, with an inch or two of water beneath, on top of a deep soup pot. Cover the top of the pot with aluminum foil to trap the steam. Or treat yourself and purchase a big pot with a steamer attachment.

Tackling a Few Techniques

The techniques of the Mexican kitchen do not call for split-second timing or finicky, precise movements. Just roll up your sleeves and get ready to chop, dice, slice, and occasionally whir the blender or sizzle foods in hot oil. Mexican cooking methods, based on techniques honed by home cooks over the years, depend only on your willingness to dive in and do the work.

Toasting and seeding vegetables and seeds

Good Mexican cooking calls for lots of roasting, toasting, and charring to give the food that mysterious deep, smoky, rustic edge. This may be the only time in your cooking career where to blacken is not only okay but preferred. Here's how to roast and toast some ingredients typically found in Mexican foods.

Fresh chiles and bell peppers

Fresh chiles and bell peppers can be roasted directly over a gas flame or on a tray under the broiler. Keep turning until the skin is evenly charred, without burning the flesh. Transfer charred peppers to a plastic bag, tie the top closed, and let the peppers sit until they're cool to the touch, about 15 minutes. (To speed things up, you can place the bag in a bowl of iced water.) Remove the blackened skin by pulling it off by hand and then dip your fingers in a bowl of water to remove any blackened bits. Once peeled, cut away stems, seeds, and veins with a paring knife.

Do not peel roasted peppers under running tap water or tasty, precious juices will be washed away.

Dried chiles

Dried chiles, like anchos, develop more flavor if lightly toasted. Just place them directly over a low gas flame or in a dry skillet over low flame and warm a few seconds on each side, until the flesh is bubbly and lightly toasted.

Vegetables

Tomatoes, tomatillos, onions, and garlic are often roasted on a tray under the broiler when making salsas, soups, and stews. Simply arrange all the vegetables to be roasted on a large baking sheet, protecting small garlic cloves by tucking them under larger vegetables. Stay nearby and keep turning the vegetables with tongs until everything is evenly blackened. Be careful to transfer the juices that collect on the baking sheet to the blender because they carry lots of delicious flavor.

You can also roast vegetables in a heavy, dry cast-iron skillet over a medium flame. Cook, turning frequently, until blackened.

Seeds

Whole coriander, cumin, and fennel seeds can be toasted on the stovetop. Place the seeds in a dry skillet over medium heat and keep shaking and tossing the pan until their aroma is released, less than a minute.

Ready, set, puree

- Never fill a blender more than halfway. Always leave a crack open at the top for steam to escape.

- Control the proportion of liquids to solids in the container by lifting solids from the pot with a spoon and then pouring a small amount of liquid from the pot to the blender. A combination of about half liquid and half solids is good.

- Always cover the top of the blender with a towel to protect yourself from escaping liquids.

- Begin the action by briefly pulsing a few times to start liquefying. When the blades are moving freely, you can let it rip.

To puree garlic in quantity, first break the bulbs apart. Peel them by first flattening the cloves with the flat side of a heavy knife or cleaver and then removing the skin. Puree with a small amount of olive oil in a blender or food processor fitted with a metal blade. Store in the refrigerator for as long as a week. Pureed garlic can always be used in place of minced garlic. One tablespoon pureed equals about 3 cloves, minced.

Welcome to the beanery

Here are some suggestions to help assure perfectly cooked beans every time:

- Never salt the water. It will toughen the bean's skin. Add salt to flavor after the beans are done.

- For maximum creaminess, always cook over low heat, with the cover on, to prevent drying.

- To prevent scorching, stir with a wooden spoon several times during cooking, always reaching down to the bottom of the pot. Burnt beans on the bottom of the pot will infuse the whole pot with their unlovely aroma.

- To test for doneness, taste a few of the smallest beans because they take the longest to cook through. If their centers are smooth and creamy, the batch is done.

- Use cool water in your sink to cool beans in a hurry.

✔ Pressure cookers are great for cooking beans. Just follow the machine's instructions.

Poppin' peppercorns for flavor

To crack peppercorns, place the whole peppercorns in the middle of a cutting board. To keep the peppercorns from flying away when you crack them, roll up a towel and use it to surround the corns. Place the heel of a skillet or saucepan on top and push down and away from you several times.

Mexican cooking light

Authentic Mexican cooking is light and healthful, with an emphasis on fresh fruits and vegetables and sauces thickened with seeds, nuts, chiles, and tortillas rather than fattening butter and cream. Mexican food's bad rap can be traced to the old Mexican-American restaurant combination platter, which was based on the concept of lots of inexpensive rice, beans, and melted cheese to accompany the margaritas.

Here are some pointers for lightening Mexican food, both at home and in restaurants:

✔ Order soft tortillas rather than crisp, fried shells.

✔ Order more *ceviches* (raw fish salads) and vegetable dishes than richer stews and cornmeal dishes.

✔ Start the meal with chips and salsa, but, once the meal is under way, hide the chips.

✔ In your own cooking, do more grilling and use strongly flavored marinades matched with salsas rather than a cooked sauce to jazz up meats and poultry.

✔ Serve a selection of vegetables, starches, grains, and protein. Divide that 16-ounce sirloin into four portions and serve it with flavorful accompaniments. It makes for much more interesting and healthful eating.

✔ If you crave crisp tortillas, try baking flour tortillas until crisp rather than frying corn tortillas.

✔ Replace that devilish sour cream or Crema in your garnishes with full-fat yogurt—equally delicious and satisfying, with hardly any calories. But don't go overboard and use nonfat yogurt. It tastes so bad that you'll end up eating more in search of some satisfaction.

Chapter 3

· · · · · · · · · ·

Stuffed Treats

The 5th Wave   By Rich Tennant

"Let me know when you've got enough lettuce on that taco."

In This Chapter

· · · · · · · · · · · · ·

▸ Snacking on savory empanadas

▸ Trying your hand at tamale making

▸ Stuffing chiles with success

· · · · · · · · · · · · ·

Mexican cooks are expert at stuffed foods. For example, they know how to make hundreds of variations of tamales. They are skilled at stuffing flavored corn masa (corn dough enriched with lard) into corn husks, banana leaves, avocado leaves, or Swiss chard. They also are adept at folding the food wrapper into an ordinary rectangle, a trickier triangle, or a giant log shape that is later served in slices. The common quality that these inventive dishes share is the element of surprise that the package creates. Opening a corn husk, inhaling the spicy aroma, and then taking a bite is intrinsically more interesting than digging into the much more obvious steak on a plate.

In Mexico, specialty cooks often sell stuffed treats in the marketplace or at street stands. Typically, a woman who is known in her village for a specific tamale or empanada sells them each day at the market. Mexicans bring home empanadas and tamales as takeout foods, just as Americans stop at a deli counter to pick up something for dinner on the way home. These stuffed treats are considered too informal to be served in restaurants in Mexico, but in the United States, a dish that requires so much work ordinarily qualifies as restaurant food.

Tamales and empanadas, with their air of mystery and delicious savor, make great party foods. And chiles rellenos is one of the best known Mexican restaurant specialties. All are so special that they don't need much to accompany them. In their homelands, stuffed treats like these that take so much care and time to make often are served at holiday feasts.

Empanadas: Little Pies Full of Flavor

If you explore your local Spanish-speaking neighborhood and wander into a few small grocery stores or bakeries, you are sure to spot a fragrant stack of *empanadas* behind the counter. Sometimes they're big overstuffed half moons, and sometimes they're delicate miniature pastries, but whatever shape they take, they have usually been crafted at home by a local cook.

With their irresistible savory fillings and neat handheld size, these little pastries are a popular snack food in most Latin American communities.

Empanadas de Picadillo

Picadillo is a dish from Spain. It contains highly seasoned, slightly sweetened, ground fried meat. In addition to making an excellent stuffing for these little turnovers, you also can use picadillo to stuff chiles for baking, to fill tacos, or to simply serve alongside rice and beans. You can make the dough recipe (which follows) a few days ahead and refrigerate it.

Special tools: *Baking sheet, pastry brush*

Preparation time: *20 minutes, plus 30 minutes chilling and 60 minutes to make the salsas*

Cooking time: *35 minutes*

Yield: *15 empanadas*

1 pound lean ground beef

1 medium yellow onion, chopped

2 cloves garlic, peeled and chopped

½ cup raisins, chopped

½ cup green olives, chopped

1 teaspoon salt

1 teaspoon pepper

2 teaspoons ground cumin

¼ teaspoon ground cloves

1 tablespoon brown sugar (optional)

½ cup Red Roasted Tomato Salsa, or store-bought salsa

Empanada Dough (see following recipe) or 1 pound frozen pie dough

1 egg combined with 2 tablespoons milk, lightly beaten for brushing on dough

Garnish: Roasted Green Chile Salsa

1 Brown the ground beef in a large heavy skillet over medium-high heat, stirring frequently, about 7 minutes. Drain off and discard the excess fat. Add the onion and sauté for 5 minutes. Then add the garlic, raisins, olives, salt, pepper, cumin, cloves, and brown sugar, if desired. Cook until their aromas are released, about 2½ minutes. Stir in the Red Roasted Tomato Salsa, bring to a boil, and set aside to cool.

2 Roll out the dough and cut into circles as described in the following recipe.

3 Place a generous tablespoon of the beef filling in the center of each pastry round. Fold over and press the edges together to seal. Transfer to a baking sheet and chill for a half hour, or wrap and freeze. (You don't have to defrost frozen empanadas before baking.)

4 Preheat the oven to 400°.

5 Brush the pastries all over with the egg wash and arrange in a single layer on a baking sheet. Bake until golden, about 15 minutes. Serve hot with the Roasted Green Chile Salsa.

For cocktail-size servings, we sometimes make empanadas into tiny bite-sized pieces. When cutting out the dough, make sure that each circle is large enough to stuff. You want each bite to contain both meat and pastry. We find a 3-inch circle is just the right size.

Empanada Dough

Feel free to substitute frozen pie dough from the supermarket for this recipe.

Preparation time: *20 minutes, plus 1 hour chilling*

2 cups flour plus additional for dusting

12 tablespoons cold butter

½ teaspoon salt

1 teaspoon sugar

¼ cup water

1 Combine the flour and butter in a large bowl. Lightly blend with your fingertips until the butter is evenly distributed in chunks. Dissolve the salt and sugar in the water and stir into the flour mixture.

2 On a lightly floured surface, turn out the mixture and lightly knead the dough until it forms a ball, adding a bit more water if necessary. Knead by pushing the ball of dough away from you with the heel of your hand, and then gathering it up, and making a quarter turn before repeating. Wrap in plastic and refrigerate for at least 1 hour or freeze as long as a week. Return to room temperature before rolling.

3 Divide the dough in half. On a floured board, roll out half the dough to a thickness of ⅛ inch. With a cookie cutter or a drinking glass, cut out 4-inch circles. Gather the scraps, add to the remaining dough, and reroll and cut out circles until all the dough is used.

Mushroom Empanadas

Mushrooms are a popular ingredient in Mexico. We love combining them with earthy corn dough rather than plain pastry, rich cheese, and a tart green salsa in these—our favorite empanadas. The trick here is to roll the dough fairly thin and make sure that the filling has plenty of oomph! Epazote, a strong-tasting wild herb, can be found in Mexican markets.

Special tool: *Baking sheet*

Preparation time: *20 minutes, plus 30 minutes refrigeration and 15 minutes to make the Green Tomatillo Salsa*

Cooking time: *20 minutes*

Yield: *16 empanaas*

2 tablespoons butter

1 small yellow onion, diced

2 cloves garlic, peeled and minced

1 pound white or oyster mushrooms, cleaned, trimmed, and coarsely chopped

1½ teaspoons salt

½ teaspoon pepper

2 arbol chiles, stemmed, seeded, and finely ground, or ½ teaspoon cayenne pepper

1 bunch epazote or parsley, leaves only, coarsely chopped (½ cup)

1 cup (4 ounces) grated ranchero or Monterey Jack cheese

1 recipe Corn Tortilla dough

¾ cup vegetable oil for frying

Garnishes: 1 cup Green Tomatillo Salsa, 1 cup shredded cabbage, and 1 cup Crema

1 Melt the butter in a medium skillet over medium heat. Sauté the onions until they just begin to brown. Then stir in the garlic and cook until the aroma is released, about 1 minute. Add the mushrooms, salt, pepper, and chiles or cayenne. Continue cooking until the mushrooms soften, about 5 minutes. Stir in the epazote and cook briefly, about 1 minute. Set aside to cool. Stir in the cheese.

2 Divide the corn tortilla dough into 16 balls and flatten, between sheets of plastic wrap, to ¼-inch-thick circles that are 3 inches in diameter. Divide the cooled mushroom mixture into 16 portions.

3 Place one portion of the mushroom mixture in the center of each circle. Fold over to enclose the filling and tightly pinch the edges together to seal. Transfer to a baking sheet, cover with plastic wrap and refrigerate for a minimum of 30 minutes or up to 2 days.

4 Pour the oil into a medium saucepan to a depth of 1 inch. Heat over medium-high heat to 375°. When the oil is hot, fry the empanadas, a few at a time, until they color slightly and rise to the surface, about 4 to 5 minutes. Transfer to paper towels to drain.

5 Split each empanada open along the seam and top with 1 tablespoon each salsa, cabbage, and Crema. Serve hot.

In making any empanada or turnover, press the edges of the dough together carefully so that no filling peeks out. Otherwise, the package can spring a leak when it's frying or baking. Another trick to keep the pastry sealed is to chill empanadas before frying them.

Tamales: Feast-Day Treats

We've tasted so many wonderful tamales in our travels, but two unusual ones really stand out. One tamale—called *brazo de reina,* or queen's arm—is an oversized tamale from the Yucatán that's made of ground pumpkin seeds and herbs mixed with masa and stuffed into a long banana leaf. We saw it served in slices for a special gathering. And the other tamale, which impressed us with its pre-Hispanic origins, was a simple tamale of rich, flavorful black beans and corn.

Wrapping a tamale

Before you can unwrap and enjoy the delicious filling of a tamale, you first need to create the tidy corn-husk packages. Just follow these steps:

1. Soak the dried corn husks in hot water for 2 hours or overnight.

2. Drain the corn husks on paper towels. Cut out 9-inch squares of aluminum foil. You'll need one for each tamale.

3. To wrap the tamales, spread 1 or 2 husks lengthwise on the counter with the narrow end pointing away from you. Spread about 2½ tablespoons of filling down the center, leaving about 2 inches bare at the top of the husk.

4. Fold over the sides and then the ends to enclose the filling. Place the folded tamale on a square of foil and fold over the foil to enclose the package. (You can also close the tamale with a strip of corn husk; see the recipe for Green Corn Tamales for instructions.) Repeat with the remaining filling and additional corn husks.

Banana leaves also make excellent wrappers for tamales. To use, holding them in your hands, run the leaves directly over a stovetop gas or electric burner on low heat or place in a dry skillet for a few seconds. This process softens the leaves, makes them fragrant, and brightens the green color. Cut them into 9-inch squares, trimming out the tough center stem, and wrap the stuffed banana leaf in foil to enclose.

Steaming the tamales

Small batches of tamales can fit into a vegetable steamer basket, but for larger quantities, you need a steamer, which is a large pot with a perforated portion on top for the tamales.

If you don't have a steamer, you can improvise by balancing a rack or colander on top of one or two empty cans or inverted coffee cups that are set in a large pasta or soup pot. Make sure that the water doesn't touch the rack's bottom.

Always keep an eye on the pot while the tamales are steaming so that the water doesn't get too low or entirely evaporate. And always line the steamer tray with extra husks to cushion the cooking process.

Tamales for every occasion

We've included some great tamale recipes for beginners in this section. Don't be daunted by a recipe's length or unfamiliar ingredients. Mastering tamale making is really just a matter of getting organized and setting aside the time, preferably with a group of friends, to dig in and cook.

Green Corn Tamales

The corn harvest is celebrated all over Latin America with different versions of these simple packets of sweet, fresh corn wrapped in corn husks. They're a good choice for the beginning tamale maker because they don't contain masa. These tamales are also a great choice for a party because everybody loves them. The flavors are simple and sweet. We've been serving them at a rapid clip for many years at our restaurants.

The green in Green Corn Tamales means that the corn is fresh rather than dried. It doesn't refer to the color of the corn, although fresh husks are green.

Special tool: *Steamer or pot fitted with a rack*

Preparation time: *15 minutes, plus 15 minutes to make the Fresh Salsa (does not include time to soften the corn husks)*

Cooking time: *1 hour and 15 minutes*

Yield: *10 to 12 tamales, or 6 servings*

3 tablespoons butter

½ cup hominy grits

3 cups canned corn, undrained (2 12-ounce cans)

½ teaspoon salt

¼ teaspoon pepper

Pinch of sugar, if necessary

½ cup milk

1 teaspoon baking powder

1 8-ounce package dried corn husks, softened

Garnishes: 1 recipe Fresh Salsa and sour cream

1 Melt the butter in a large skillet over moderate heat. Add the grits and cook for about 4 minutes, until golden. Add the corn and its juices, the salt, pepper, the sugar if the corn isn't sweet, and the milk, and simmer until the mixture is thick as oatmeal, about 7 minutes. Set aside to cool until touchable. Then stir in the baking powder and reserve in the refrigerator.

2 Wrap the tamales in corn husks according to the instructions in "Wrapping a tamale" earlier in this chapter. You can skip the step of wrapping the package in foil. Instead, make ties for the tamales by cutting a few of the moistened husks into 6 by ¼-inch strips. Use the strips to tie the "package" closed with a double knot.

3 In a steamer or a pot fitted with a rack, make a bed for the tamales by laying the remaining corn husks on the bottom of the rack. Layer the tamales upright and steam over low heat for 1 hour. Remove from the steamer and let rest 10 minutes. Serve hot with the garnishes in bowls at the table.

For sweetened fresh corn tamales, add ½ teaspoon ground cinnamon, ¼ teaspoon cloves, ¼ teaspoon nutmeg, and ½ cup raisins to the skillet when you add the corn. For a savory touch and some color, stir roasted and diced red or green bell peppers into the corn.

Celebrate your own corn harvest by substituting 10 ears of fresh corn, with the kernels scraped off the cob and uncooked, in the Green Corn Tamales. Add about ½ cup cream. Save the green husks for wrapping, and then you'll realize how these tamales got their name.

Basic Masa Tamales with Fillings

Our basic masa tamale recipe is built for flexibility. First, we explain the technique for beating the masa, filling the corn husks, and then steaming. We follow that recipe with four options for savory fillings to flavor the masa—chiles and cheese, chicken and salsa, pork in adobo sauce, and left-over mole.

The salsas or sauces that go with the fillings are used in three ways: ½ cup gets beaten into the masa, ½ cup gets mixed into the filling, and the remaining ½ cup is served with the finished tamales.

Tamales as delicious as these deserve to be the main focus of a meal. The traditional accompaniments are rice and beans, but we prefer to serve them with something lighter. A trio of interesting salads, like the Fiesta Bean, Cactus Paddle, and Caesar Salads would be terrific, as would any big green salad.

You can store leftover tamales in the refrigerator as long as 4 days, or you can freeze them. Reheat for about 30 minutes in the steamer.

Special tools: *Electric mixer, steamer or pot fitted with a rack*

Preparation time: *30 minutes (not including the preparation time for the filling and sauce and softening time for corn husks)*

Cooking time: *1 hour and 15 minutes (not including the preparation time for the filling and sauce)*

Yield: *12 to 14 tamales*

½ cup sauce from one of the filling recipes that follow this recipe

1 cup chicken stock, at room temperature

1 teaspoon baking soda

1½ teaspoons salt

1 pound cold prepared ground masa for tamales, or 1¾ cup dry masa harina, moistened with 1 cup warm water and then chilled

½ cup vegetable shortening or cold lard

1 8-ounce package dried corn husks, softened

Fillings and sauces (see the following recipes)

Garnish: Sour cream

1 Mix together ½ cup of the salsa or sauce from one of the fillings, the chicken stock, baking soda, and salt and set aside.

2 Place the masa in the bowl of an electric mixer and beat at medium speed until light in texture, about 6 minutes. Slowly add the chicken stock mixture while beating continuously at medium-high speed. Turn the mixer speed up to high and add the shortening or lard, a tablespoon at a time, beating well after each addition. Continue beating and scraping down the bowl until the mixture is light and fluffy, about 15 minutes total. Test for lightness by dropping 1 tablespoon of masa into cold water: If it floats, the mixture is light enough. If not, continue beating at high speed a few minutes longer.

3 Wrap the tamales according to the instructions in "Wrapping a tamale" earlier in this chapter, spreading about 2½ tablespoons of the masa mixture over a 2-by-3-inch area of husk. Top with a spoonful of filling and its sauce.

4 To cook, line a steamer with corn husks and fill with tamales, upright in layers. Cook over simmering water for 1 hour and 15 minutes, until the husks just pull away from the masa without sticking. Serve hot with the remaining sauce and sour cream. (Cold tamales can be reheated in a steamer over simmering water for 30 minutes.)

Green Chile Cheese Filling

If you like chile rellenos, you'll love this similar combination of roasted green chiles and luscious rich cheese. It's amazing that all it takes is a great cheese and a great salsa to make a terrific tamale.

Preparation time: *15 minutes, plus 15 minutes to make the Green Tomatillo Salsa*

Yield: *12 to 14 tamales*

1½ cups Green Tomatillo Salsa

4 poblano chiles, roasted, peeled, seeded, and cut into ½-inch strips

1 pound Mexican cheese, such as Ranchero, queso fresco, panela, or manchego, cut into ½-inch cubes (about 3 cups)

In a large mixing bowl, combine ½ cup of the salsa, the chiles, and the cheese. (Reserve ½ cup of the salsa to incorporate into the masa.) Serve the remaining ½ cup of salsa alongside the finished tamales.

Roasted Tomato Chicken Filling

Olives and raisins add sweet and salty accents to this easy chicken filling.

Preparation time: *5 minutes, plus 35 minutes to make the Red Roasted Tomato Salsa*

Cooking time: *15 minutes*

Yield: *12 to 14 tamales*

1½ cups Red Roasted Tomato Salsa	*½ cup green olives, pitted*
2 cups shredded cooked chicken	*½ cup golden raisins*

In a medium saucepan over medium heat, combine ½ cup of the salsa, the chicken, olives, and raisins. Simmer for about 15 minutes, until heated through. (Reserve ½ cup of the salsa to incorporate into the masa.) Serve the remaining ½ cup salsa alongside the finished tamales.

Pork and Green Chile Adobo Filling

Rich pork and spicy green chiles on a steaming bed of corn masa are a tough combination to beat.

Preparation time: *5 minutes, plus 1 hour 20 minutes to make the Adobo Sauce*

Cooking time: *15 minutes*

Yield: *12 to 14 tamales*

1½ cups Adobo Sauce	*1 poblano chile, roasted, peeled, seeded and cut into ½-inch wide strips*
2 cups shredded, cooked pork	

In a medium saucepan over medium heat, combine ½ cup of the Adobo Sauce, the pork, and the chile. Simmer for about 15 minutes, until heated through. (Reserve ½ cup of the sauce to incorporate into the masa.) Serve the remaining ½ cup sauce alongside the finished tamales.

Chicken Mole Filling

Serve these festive, rich tamales at holiday time when you need a make-ahead menu for a buffet.

Preparation time: *5 minutes, plus 2 hours 10 minutes to make the Mole Sauce*

Cooking time: *15 minutes*

Yield: *12 to 14 tamales*

1½ cups Mole Sauce or store-bought mole sauce

1½ cups cooked shredded meat from mole recipe

In a medium saucepan over medium heat, combine ½ cup of the mole and the shredded meat. Simmer for about 15 minutes, until heated through. (Reserve ½ cup of the mole to incorporate into the masa.) Serve the remaining ½ cup of mole alongside the finished tamales.

Chiles Rellenos

If your guests are full-fledged chile fanatics, you can't go wrong with a dish featuring whole stuffed chiles, known as *chiles rellenos* (CHEE-lehs reh-YEH-nohs).

Both of the recipes in this section are a bit fancier than tamales or empanadas (they are sit-down, rather than stand-up, foods). But, like other stuffed treats, they also derive much of their savor from the blending that occurs when a food is wrapped and then cooked. The edible wrapper, in this case the smoky, roasted poblano, seals in and intensifies the flavor of the stuffing, while its own juices soak in and enrich the final product.

Classic Chiles Rellenos

These crisply coated, deep-fried chiles are a standby at any good Mexican restaurant. Stuffed chiles can be made and refrigerated up to a day in advance for easy preparation. If you find the filling too rich, feel free to add some other vegetables like corn kernels or peas to the cheese.

Special tool: *Baking sheet*

Preparation time: *45 minutes, plus 50 minutes to make the salsas*

Cooking time: *30 minutes*

Yield: *4 servings, 8 chiles*

3 cups (12 ounces) grated Mexican manchego or Monterey Jack cheese

½ cup (2 ounces) grated panela cheese

½ cup (2 ounces) grated añejo cheese

8 medium poblano chiles, roasted and peeled
⅓ cup flour for coating the chiles

4 eggs, separated

½ teaspoon salt

½ teaspoon pepper

Vegetable oil for frying

1 cup Red Roasted Tomato Salsa

1 cup Green Tomatillo Salsa

Garnish: 6 tablespoons Crema

1 Combine the cheeses in a large bowl and divide into 8 equal portions.

2 With a sharp paring knife, carefully make a lengthwise slit in each chile. Cut out and discard the stems, seeds, and veins. Mold the cheese mixture portions into torpedo shapes and place one inside each chile. Roll each chile to completely enclose the cheese and reserve in the refrigerator for up to 8 hours.

3 Preheat the oven to 350°.

4 On a counter near the stovetop, spread the flour on a plate or a piece of wax paper. In a clean bowl, whisk the egg whites with the salt until stiff. In another large, wide mixing bowl, beat the yolks with the pepper until smooth. Fold the beaten whites into the yolks and place near the flour.

5 Dip each stuffed chile in the flour, taking care to coat completely. Thoroughly pat off any excess flour with your hands.

6 Pour about 1 inch of vegetable oil into a wide cast-iron skillet. Place over moderate heat until almost smoking, about 350°. Dip two chiles at a time in the beaten eggs and roll them around in the eggs until entirely coated. (No green should be showing.)

7 Gently lift the chiles out with the palm of your hand, one at a time, and holding your hand just above the oil, slide the chile into the pan. Fry until lightly browned, and then turn with a slotted spoon and brown the other side. Lift from the oil with a slotted spoon and drain on a paper towel-lined baking sheet. When all 8 chiles are cooked, remove the paper and transfer to the oven for 5 minutes or until the cheese is entirely melted.

8 To serve, coat 4 plates with half red and half green salsa and place 2 chiles on each plate. Top with Crema and serve immediately.

Because roasted peppers are slippery to handle, at our restaurants we place the chiles on a kitchen towel for easier rolling.

Finding poblano chiles for stuffing is worth the search. Not only do they have the best flavor, but their wide shoulders and thick flesh make them easier for stuffing. Remember that a chile's spiciness varies according to growing conditions.

Corn-and-Cheese-Stuffed Chiles in Red Rice

You can avoid last-minute jitters by putting the casserole together in the morning or the night before and then just placing it in the oven right before your guests arrive.

Preparation time: *15 minutes, plus 35 minutes to make the Red Roasted Tomato Salsa, 20 minutes to roast the chiles, and 50 minutes to make the rice*

Cooking time: *35 minutes*

Yield: *6 servings*

4 tablespoons butter or oil

1 medium yellow onion, chopped

2 cloves garlic, peeled and minced

3 cups fresh or thawed frozen corn kernels (about 6 ears fresh corn or 2 10-ounce packages, frozen)

1½ teaspoons coarse salt

1 teaspoon pepper

1 cup (4 ounces) grated manchego or Monterey Jack cheese

*6 large poblano chiles, roasted and peeled
4 cups cooked white rice*

1 cup Crema

1 cup Red Roasted Tomato Salsa

½ cup (2 ounces) grated añejo cheese

1 Preheat the oven to 350°.

2 Melt the butter in a medium saucepan over medium heat. Sauté the onion for about 5 minutes until translucent. Add the garlic and cook for 1 minute longer. Add the corn, salt, and pepper, and sauté until tender, about 2½ minutes. Transfer to a bowl and cool. Stir in the manchego or Monterey Jack cheese and set aside.

3 Carefully slit the chiles lengthwise, removing the seeds and veins, leaving the stems and tops intact if possible. Stuff the chiles with the corn mixture.

4 Arrange the rice in a shallow buttered roasting pan or casserole. Nestle the chiles in the rice in a single layer. Mix together the Crema and Red Roasted Tomato Salsa and pour over all. Sprinkle with the añejo cheese and transfer to the oven. Bake for about 25 minutes, until heated through. Serve hot.

In any stuffed chile dish, start with well-roasted chiles. If they are not thoroughly roasted, they won't be pliable, which makes stuffing the chiles difficult, plus you'll miss out on the important roasted flavor.

Chapter 4

• • • • • • • • • • •

Soulful Soups and Border Salads

The 5th Wave   By Rich Tennant

"Now THIS is authentic Mexican cooking. The beans in this dish came from a fresh pair of maracas I picked up this afternoon."

In This Chapter

• • • • • • • • • • • • • • • •

▸ Making soup, Mexican style

▸ Hearing the garnishing truth

▸ Stock-making and freezing tips

▸ Getting your greens ready to go

▸ Serving a salad sandwich (The tostada)

▸ Adding new dimensions to your food with side salads

• • • • • • • • • • • • • • • • •

Any large cylindrical pot will do for making Mexican soup, but here are some pointers if you're in the market for a new pot:

- ✔ Bigger is better when choosing pots for making soup. If you're going to splurge on a new stockpot, go for the 12-quart size for maximum versatility. You may never fill a large pot, but the good news is that you'll rarely have to worry about overflows onto your sparkly clean stovetop.

- ✔ Aluminum is fine for a soup pot. It conducts heat well and is less expensive than stainless steel. Just make sure that the pot is heavy-bottomed or lined with copper on the bottom so that it doesn't warp over time.

- ✔ You want a soup pot to be heavy, but not too heavy. A 12-quart pot made of enameled cast-iron could be a problem to lift once it's full of liquid.

- ✔ Handles on either side for easy lifting and a tight-fitting lid are lovely features of a soup pot.

And don't forget to have a ladle—the stockpot's best friend—for gracefully transferring liquids.

Discovering the art of the garnish

As chefs, we've had to face the cold hard facts. Probably some people do not follow our recipes exactly, especially when it comes to that long list of garnishes at the end of our soup recipes. Some of you may even ignore garnishing altogether—a thought we prefer not to entertain.

Here's how we feel about garnishes: All these soups can be served without any garnish—they will still taste terrific. We develop the garnishes to enhance the look of a dish and add contrasting tastes and textures. The garnish elevates the soup from something simple to something exquisite. To us, garnishes are so integral to the dish that it pains us to see people garnishing improperly. We add salsa to earthy bean soup for a fresh note of acidity and a bright dash of color, and we arrange strips of avocado on lime soup to mellow out the acidity. And garnishes of corn chips add crunch to many types of soup.

At home, we know that you need to stay flexible so that cooking isn't a chore. Use the garnishes you have on hand and substitute where possible.

Freezing soups

Most soups are ideal for freezing. You can make soup whenever you have the time and then freeze it and serve it later—without any loss of quality.

A squirt of lime

The one ingredient essential to Mexican soup making is that final wedge of lime, squirted and then tossed into the bowl right before serving. That splash of fresh acidity freshens all the other flavors and brings them up a note. Try a wedge of lime in your next winter vegetable soup or bowl of chili for a Mexican twist.

It's best to cool a pot of soup down before storing it in your freezer or refrigerator so that the heat from the soup doesn't lower the temperature inside the freezer.

Here's an easy way to cool your soup: Fill a sink with iced water and lower the hot pot into it. Stir occasionally until the entire soup is cool to the touch. Then store the soup in plastic containers, with an inch of air at the top, and freeze as long as 2 months.

Creating your own stock

If you want to taste the difference between good and great, compare a soup made with homemade stock with a soup made with canned stock or bouillon cubes.

Good stock recipes are available in any all-purpose cookbook, but here are some general guidelines for the two we use most often.

Chicken stock

To make about 3 quarts (12 cups) of chicken stock, just follow these steps:

1. **Combine about 2½ pounds chicken bones (or backs and wings, including turkey wings, with the meat attached are great), 1 coarsely chopped celery stalk, 1 onion, and 2 carrots in a stockpot.**

2. **Add enough water to cover generously, along with ½ bunch fresh or 1 tablespoon dried parsley or thyme, 1 tablespoon salt, ½ tablespoon peppercorns, and 4**

bay leaves.

3. Bring to a boil, reduce to a simmer, and cook, uncovered, about 1½ hours. Check the pot occasionally and skim and discard the foam from the top.

4. Let the stock cool in the pot and then pour through a strainer, discarding the solids.

You can store this chicken stock in sealed containers in the refrigerator for up to 5 days or in the freezer as long as 3 months. Remove the layer of fat from the top and discard, or save for sautéing.

Vegetable stock

To make about 2½ quarts (10 cups) vegetable stock, follow these steps:

1. Combine chopped vegetables such as 2 onions, 1 parsnip, 2 celery ribs, 2 carrots, and 1 fennel bulb in a large pot. Add 2 chopped tomatoes, 6 corn cobs (without the kernels), 6 garlic cloves, 1 bunch of parsley or thyme, 2 bay leaves, 3 cloves, and plenty of black peppercorns and salt.

2. Add enough water to cover, bring to a boil, reduce to a simmer, and cook, uncovered, about 1½ hours. Check the pot occasionally and skim and discard the foam from the top.

3. Let the soup cool in the pot and then pour through a strainer, discarding the solids.

Using canned stocks

When you just don't have the time or energy to make stock from scratch, use canned chicken or vegetable broth and add some water to dilute the salty taste.

The typical can of chicken broth contains 14½ ounces, so, by pouring the contents of the can into a 2 cup measure and then adding water to the 2 cup level, you can get about 2 cups of stock from each can.

Soup is for tasting

Taste, taste, taste your soup before adjusting seasonings with salt and pepper at the end of the cooking time. The saltiness of any finished soup depends on the saltiness of the broth you used for cooking. Because canned stock and bouillon cubes are quite salty to begin with, and boiling intensifies flavors, you may not need salt at all at the end of cooking.

So Many Sopas, So Little Time

Mexican cooks make several types of brothy dishes, but the most popular are the thinner broths referred to as *sopas* (Spanish for "soups"). They run the gamut from rich creamed vegetable soups, to cold gazpacho, to the thin and familiar tortilla soup, but the unifying thread is that all are light enough to be eaten as a first course.

Sopa secas are leftover sopas in which the liquid has been absorbed enough for the dish to be eaten as a side dish or starter, with a fork.

Tangy Cold Avocado Soup

We don't often use water in our soup making, but this velvety green soup doesn't need the enhancement of a stock. It is full of flavor and richness from the avocado and has just the right note of tartness from the tomatillos. This is a good dish to make in the summertime when your avocados are just the other side of ripe.

Special tool: *Blender or food processor*

Preparation time: *15 minutes*

Yield: *6 servings (8 cups)*

8 tomatillos, roughly chopped (about 2 cups)

2 jalapeño chiles, roasted and seeded

Juice of 1 lime (2 tablespoons)

Juice of ½ orange (¼ cup)

1 teaspoon salt

½ teaspoon black pepper

1 cup cold water plus enough ice cubes to bring water to 2 cups in a liquid measure

2 ripe avocados, peeled and seeded

Garnish: 1 bunch scallions, thinly sliced (⅔ cup)

Combine the tomatillos, jalapeños, lime and orange juices, salt, pepper, and a tablespoon or two of the ice water in a blender or food processor. Puree until smooth. Add the avocados with the remaining water mixture and puree briefly, just until smooth. Serve in chilled bowls with the scallions scattered on top.

Watch that trigger finger when you push the puree button! This recipe calls for just a few seconds or pulses. Lengthy processing incorporates too much air, giving the soup a frothy head, which is great for a beer but not desirable in a soup.

To accessorize this acidy green soup for a party, try a dollop of your favorite red salsa in the center or, better yet, drizzle it freehand from a spoon. Chopped tomatoes or strips of roasted red pepper also add a nice spot of color. Or for a lovely rich, green salad dressing, omit the ice cubes and use less water—about ½ cup.

Tomatillo and Chicken Chilaquiles

Chilaquiles (chee-lah-KEE-lehs), a homey dish of day-old tortillas and salsa, is eaten all over Mexico as a hearty breakfast or light midday meal. This version is wet enough to serve as a soup, but if you wait a day, the tortillas absorb enough liquid to turn it into a sopa seca, or dry soup.

This recipe provides a great use for leftover chicken meat. Just start the cooking at Step 2 with ½ pound of cooked, shredded chicken.

Preparation time: *10 minutes, plus 15 minutes for the Green Tomatillo Salsa*

Cooking time: *30 minutes*

Yield: *4 servings*

6 cups chicken stock

½ pound boneless, skinless chicken breasts

Salt and pepper to taste

2 tablespoons vegetable oil

1 medium yellow onion, thinly sliced

3 cloves garlic, crushed and peeled

2 cups Green Tomatillo Salsa

7 small (6-inch) corn tortillas, or about 3 dozen tortilla chips

½ bunch cilantro leaves, chopped (½ cup)

Garnishes: ¼ cup (1 ounce) grated añejo cheese, ½ cup diced onion, and ½ cup Crema

1 Bring the chicken stock to a boil in a deep skillet. Sprinkle the chicken breasts with salt and pepper and add to the stock. Simmer, covered, for 8 to 10 minutes. (Don't boil the stock to avoid toughening the meat.)

2 Remove the chicken breasts from the skillet, wrap them in a damp tea towel, and set aside to cool. When they're cool enough to handle, shred the chicken into long strips. Reserve the stock.

3 Heat the oil in a stockpot over medium heat. Sauté the onion with salt and pepper until soft. Add the garlic and cook for about 3 minutes, until the aroma is released. Add the salsa and bring to a boil. Pour in the reserved chicken stock and simmer for 10 minutes.

4 Cut fresh tortillas into ½-inch strips and fry according to the instructions in chapter 5.

5 Add the shredded chicken to the stock pot and season with salt and pepper. Bring to a boil and stir in the cilantro and fried tortilla strips or chips. Simmer 5 minutes longer. Ladle into 4 bowls. Garnish with the cheese, onion, and a dollop of Crema. Serve hot.

For breakfast chilaquiles, top each serving with a fried egg.

Gazpacho

Gazpacho is a perfect first course for just about anything you choose to serve in the heat of the summer—except for a tomato-based entrée.

Gazpacho is one of those simple uncooked dishes where a quality olive oil makes a great deal of difference. So haul out that expensive extra-virgin olive oil you got as a present for your last birthday and let it pour. You won't regret it.

This soup keeps in the refrigerator up to 2 days.

Special tool: *Blender or food processor*

Preparation time: *20 minutes, plus 2 hours chilling time*

Yield: *4 to 6 servings*

1 slice white bread, crusts removed	*½ cup extra-virgin olive oil*
2 tablespoons red wine vinegar	*3 jalapeño chiles, stemmed, seeded, and chopped*
3 cups tomato juice, plus more if needed to thin the soup	*1 teaspoon sugar*
6 pickling cucumbers, peeled, seeded, and diced	*¾ teaspoon salt*
	½ teaspoon black pepper
4 scallions, thinly sliced	*Garnish: Sliced chives*
1 red bell pepper, seeded and diced	
2 cloves garlic, peeled	

1 Place the bread on a plate, sprinkle it with the vinegar, and let sit until thoroughly moistened, 5 minutes.

2 Combine the tomato juice, cucumbers, scallions, and red pepper in a large bowl.

3 Transfer about one-fourth of the vegetable mixture to a blender or food processor. Add the moistened bread, garlic, olive oil, jalapeños, sugar, salt, and pepper. Puree until smooth.

4 Pour the puree into the bowl with the vegetables. Stir to combine. Thin with more tomato juice if desired and adjust seasonings. Chill for at least 2 hours. Serve cold and garnish with chives.

Because the taste of tomato juice is so dominant in Gazpacho, the juice you choose is important. As a serious tomato juice sipper, I advise you to read the labels carefully before purchasing a juice. Briskly reject any juices with weird ancillary ingredients. If nature intended bisulfates to be in tomato juice, she would have put them in tomatoes. Don't even think about buying any tomato juices containing sugar or Bloody Mary spices. No way—not in this delicious soup. Tomatoes and salt are all you really want to see on that label.

To turn this refreshing soup into a meal, try placing a pile of cold Aztecan Quinoa Salad in the center of a shallow soup bowl and pouring the soup around it. At the restaurant, we mold the quinoa in a *timbale* (a small ceramic mold) or custard cup and invert it onto the dish for a more polished look. If you like rice in your soup, you'll love this soup and grain combination.

Corn and Chile Chowder

To make the Corn and Chile Chowder or any milk-based soup in advance and freeze, cook until the end of Step 1. Then freeze. To defrost and finish, warm the corn mixture in a soup pot and continue the recipe at Step 2.

Special tool: *Blender or food processor*

Preparation time: *20 minutes*

Cooking time: *40 minutes*

Yield: *4 to 6 servings (6 cups)*

2 tablespoons olive oil

1 medium yellow onion, diced

1 teaspoon salt

4 cups fresh or canned corn kernels, drained (8 ears fresh corn, 2½ 12-ounce cans, or 3 10-ounce packages, frozen)

2 to 3 cloves garlic, peeled and minced

1 teaspoon ground cumin

3 poblano or Anaheim chiles, roasted, peeled, seeded, and diced

2 cups milk or half-and-half

2 cups chicken stock

Garnish: ½ bunch chives, thinly sliced diagonally (¼ cup)

1 Heat the olive oil in a large stockpot over medium heat. Sauté the onion with the salt until golden brown, about 15 minutes. Add the corn, turn the heat to high, and cook for 5 to 7 minutes, until slightly browned. Stir in the garlic and cumin and cook, stirring frequently, 2 minutes longer. Reduce the heat to low, stir in the chiles, and cook for 2 to 3 more minutes.

2 Pour in the milk and chicken stock. Bring to a simmer over low heat, being careful not to boil. Gently simmer, uncovered, for 15 minutes.

3 Pour one-third of the soup into a food processor or blender and puree. Stir back into the stock pot and simmer for 5 minutes longer. Serve hot, garnished with chives.

If you can't get your hands on the more exotic chiles, substitute 2 green bell peppers and 2 jalapeño chiles, both roasted and diced.

Tortilla Soup

Tortilla soup, probably the best-known of the Mexican soups, is a brilliant use of two common Mexican leftovers—tortillas and salsa.

If you don't feel like making the Red Roasted Tomato Salsa first, you can substitute a favorite bottled smooth red salsa. You can also simply puree the following ingredients in the blender: 1½ pounds of Roma tomatoes, 6 cloves garlic, 1 small yellow onion, and ½ cup water and add to the pot along with the stock.

Preparation time: *15 minutes, plus 15 minutes for Red Roasted Tomato Salsa*

Cooking time: *1 hour*

Yield: *6 servings*

3 tablespoons olive oil

1 large yellow onion, diced

3 cloves garlic, peeled and minced

2 cups Red Roasted Tomato Salsa

5 cups chicken stock (see the "Chicken stock" section in this chapter)

1 dried chipotle chile, stemmed and seeded (optional)

1 teaspoon salt

¾ pound fried tortilla chips

Garnishes: 1 bunch cilantro leaves (½ cup); 1 avocado, peeled, seeded, and coarsely chopped; ½ cup Crema; 2 limes, cut in wedges

1 Heat the olive oil in a large stockpot over low heat. Add the onion and cook, stirring frequently, until pale brown and caramelized, 10 to 15 minutes. Stir in the garlic and cook 10 minutes longer.

2 Pour in the tomato salsa, chicken stock, chipotle chile (if desired), and salt. Bring to a boil, reduce to a simmer, and cook, uncovered, for 20 minutes. Stir in the fried tortilla chips and cook 10 minutes longer, until the chips soften. Remove and discard the chile. Serve hot, topped with cilantro, avocado, Crema, and lime wedges.

Toasted Angel Hair Soup

In this classic soup, called *fideo* (fee-DEH-oh) in Spanish, the noodles are toasted to bring a typical Mexican smokiness to the broth. You can use any thin pasta in small pieces.

Special tool: *Blender*

Preparation time: *10 minutes*

Cooking time: *30 minutes*

Yield: *6 servings*

⅓ cup olive oil

8 ounces dried angel hair pasta, broken into 1-inch pieces

3 dried chipotle chiles

1½ pounds Roma tomatoes

6 cloves garlic, peeled

1 medium yellow onion, coarsely chopped

½ cup water

2 teaspoons salt

6 cups chicken or vegetable stock

Garnishes: 1 avocado, peeled, seeded, and sliced, and 1 bunch chopped cilantro leaves (½ cup)

1 Heat the olive oil in a large stockpot over medium-low heat. Sauté the pasta, stirring frequently, until golden brown, being careful not to burn. Then stir in the chiles and cook for 2 minutes longer.

2 Meanwhile, combine the tomatoes, garlic, onion, water, and salt in a blender. Puree until smooth.

3 Add the tomato puree and chicken or vegetable stock to the stockpot. Bring to a boil and reduce to a simmer. Cook until the noodles soften and the flavors meld, about 15 minutes. Remove and discard the whole chiles. Serve hot, garnished with avocado and cilantro.

To totally demystify Toasted Angel Hair Soup, which is my favorite Mexican soup, I like to describe it as Mexican Chicken Noodle Soup. It's similar to brand-name soups but just a bit deeper and spicier.

Do not, we repeat, *do not* shortchange the all-important sautéing step at the beginning of this recipe. If you do, you might as well be eating any old chicken noodle soup. Susan will be disappointed. Anyway, you bought a Mexican cookbook to cook Mexican style, and that's what the browning step is all about.

Creamed Summer Squash Soup

Smooth creamed soups, such as this lovely one for summer, aren't often associated with the Mexican-American kitchen. But in Mexico they are common and delicious first courses.

Special tools: *Blender or food processor, strainer*

Preparation time: *10 minutes*

Cooking time: *40 minutes*

Yield: *8 servings (8 cups)*

4 tablespoons butter

1 large yellow onion, sliced

1 teaspoon salt

½ teaspoon black pepper

2 cloves garlic, peeled and sliced

6 cups vegetable stock or water

1 pound small zucchini or pattypan squash, thinly sliced

2 cups half-and-half

Salt and pepper to taste

Garnishes: ½ cup (2 ounces) grated añejo cheese and 1 lime, cut in wedges

1 Melt the butter in a stockpot over moderate heat. Sauté the onion with the salt and pepper for about 5 minutes. Add the garlic and cook 1 to 2 minutes longer. Pour in the vegetable stock or water. Bring to a boil, reduce to a simmer, and cook for 10 minutes. Stir in the squash and cook for 5 minutes longer.

2 Transfer the soup to a blender or food processor and puree until smooth. Strain back into the stockpot. Add the half-and-half and bring to a boil. Season with salt and pepper. Serve hot, garnished with the cheese and the lime wedges.

To cut calories, use half the butter called for in the recipe and substitute 1 percent nonfat milk for the half-and-half. If you garden or visit a farmer's market in the summer, you may want to try this soup with the flowers of the zucchini plant, or zucchini blossoms, as it might be made in Oaxaca; the flavor of flowers is like essence of zucchini. Substitute about 8 cups of flowers for the zucchini or squash, and use the flowers exactly as you would the squash. Carefully open and examine blooms for bugs before cooking.

I'll try almost anything once, but when it comes to bugs, I pass. Always rinse all fruits and vegetables well to remove any garden critters before cooking.

Pinto Bean Soup with Fresh Salsa

This wholesome bean soup doesn't contain a lot of distractions. It derives its creamy, luxurious texture from the beans themselves. If you don't have time to make the Fresh Salsa, bottled salsa will do just fine.

Special tool: *Blender*

Preparation time: *15 minutes*

Cooking time: *1½ hours for beans, plus an additional 45 minutes*

Yield: *8 servings (8 cups)*

1½ cups dry pinto beans	*Salt and pepper to taste*
7 cups water	*3 cloves garlic, peeled and minced*
¼ cup olive oil	*6 cups chicken or vegetable stock or water*
1½ medium yellow onions, diced	*Garnishes: Fresh Salsa and Crema*

1 Combine the beans and water in a large pot over high heat and bring to a boil. Reduce to a simmer and cook, covered, until the beans are tender but still firm, about 1 hour and 15 minutes. Stir the pot occasionally. Remove from heat.

2 In another large saucepan, heat the olive oil over medium heat. Sauté the onions with the salt and pepper until lightly browned, about 10 minutes. Then add the garlic and cook a few minutes longer. Add beans and their liquid, and the stock or additional water. Bring to a boil and reduce to a simmer. Cook, uncovered, stirring occasionally, 25 minutes longer.

3 Transfer to a blender and puree in batches until smooth. Return to the pot and warm over low heat, stirring frequently, until ready to serve. Serve hot with the salsa and Crema as garnish.

Boiling the beans before soup making replaces the overnight soaking stage that a lot of old bean recipes call for. After the beans have been softened by boiling, you can set them aside in their water and cook the soup a few hours later or the next day. Refrigerate the beans if saving them overnight.

Bean soups need lots of stirring so that the same beans don't sit at the bottom and scorch, so stay nearby.

The Caldo Connection

Caldos (KAHL-dohs) are hearty broths filled with large enough chunks of meats and vegetables to make them a meal. Chicken soup, or *caldo de pollo* (KAHL-doh deh POH-yoh), is often such a light meal, eaten with toasted tortillas. What could be finer than a nice, bubbling hot caldo waiting on the stove after a day spent outdoors in the cold?

Lime Soup

If chicken soup can cure a cold, then this bracing chicken and lime broth from the Yucatán is like a double dose of goodness.

When we first tasted this caldo, called Sopa de Lima in Mexico, it made such a big impression on us that we knew we had to re-create it at home.

Special tool: *Strainer*

Preparation time: *15 minutes*

Cooking time: *1 hour and 10 minutes*

Yield: *6 to 8 servings*

1 2-pound chicken, cut into medium pieces

12 cups chicken stock (see the "Chicken stock" section in this chapter)

2½ teaspoons salt

1½ teaspoons black peppercorns, cracked

1½ teaspoons dried oregano

½ head garlic (8 cloves), separated and crushed (unpeeled)

2 tablespoons olive oil

1 medium yellow onion, halved and sliced

Black pepper to taste

1 poblano or Anaheim chile, cored, seeded, and julienned

2 medium tomatoes, cored, seeded, and julienned

Juice of 3 limes (½ cup)

Garnishes: 3 limes, cut in wedges; 3 serrano chiles, seeded and minced; 1 cup crushed corn chips; 1 avocado, peeled, seeded, and chopped

1 Combine the chicken and stock in a large stockpot. Bring to a boil and skim and discard the foam. Add 1½ teaspoons of the salt, the cracked peppercorns, oregano, and garlic. Reduce to a simmer and cook for 35 minutes, until the meat is tender. Remove the chicken, transfer to a platter, and cover with a damp tea towel.

2 Strain the stock, discarding the solids. Skim and discard the layer of fat that settles on the top.

3 When the chicken is cool enough to handle, remove the skin and pull the meat from the bones. Shred the meat into strips and set aside.

4 Heat the olive oil in a large stockpot over medium-low heat. Cook the onion with the remaining 1 teaspoon salt and ground pepper until translucent, about 10 minutes. Stir in the chile and cook for 5 minutes longer. Add the tomatoes, shredded chicken, reserved chicken stock, and lime juice. Bring to a boil, reduce to a simmer, and cook, uncovered, for 12 minutes. Serve hot with the garnishes scattered on top.

A caldo such as this lends itself to innumerable variations. For example, you can add large chunks of peeled potato, carrot, and chayote to the broth at the end and simmer for about 20 minutes. Or if you like some rice in your chicken soup, add about ½ cup of leftover rice along with the chicken.

To re-create the taste of Seville oranges, try combining the juices of grapefruit, orange, and lime in a ratio of 2 tablespoons grapefruit juice, to 1 tablespoon orange juice, to 2 tablespoons lime juice. Try it in place of the lime juice in Lime Soup for a taste of the real thing.

Possibly the Best Posole

Posoles, more like stews than soups, are even heartier than caldos, thanks to the key starch ingredient of hominy, a form of corn (see the sidebar for more on hominy). These heavy hitters are a whole meal—like a crunchy salad served over a thick meaty broth. See the variations in this section for posole possibilities.

Homily on hominy

You can find canned hominy in the international or canned vegetable section of the supermarket. Hominy is made from dried white field corn that has been cooked with powdered lime until its skin falls off. Then the kernels' eyes are removed, and the kernel blossoms—resembling a moist piece of popped corn.

Chicken Posole

Although there is no one correct way to cook a posole, traditionally this stewy dish contains pork and hominy. However, because southern Californians prefer their meat white, we created this lighter version for our restaurant. We did draw the line, however, at breast meat. Dark thighs and legs are so much tastier.

If you don't have time to prepare all the garnishes, don't be deterred. The most important ones are fresh crunchy onions, lime, and oregano.

You can make posole (except for the garnishes) in advance and freeze it. Prepare the garnishes while the soup is reheating.

Special tools: *Blender, strainer*

Preparation time: *20 minutes*

Cooking time: *1½ hours*

Yield: *8 servings (10 cups)*

The orange of Seville

In the Yucatán peninsula, where Sopa de Lima (Lime Soup) comes from, it isn't made from limes but with Seville oranges—the same oranges used to make the famous marmalade from Spain.

Also known as bitter oranges or *naranja agria*, this small fruit has thick, green, bumpy skin and is less juicy than an ordinary orange. Its potent sour juice replaces vinegar in typical Yucatecan marinades and seasoning pastes. Although bitter oranges are also found in Puerto Rico and Cuba, only Mexicans prize the juice more than the fleshy skin. At Mexican markets, the fruit is sold with the top layer of skin removed so that the bitter oils don't seep into the juice.

1 pound boneless, skinless chicken thighs, cut in 1-inch cubes

½ teaspoon salt

4 cups water

4 ancho chiles, stemmed and seeded

5 cloves garlic, peeled

1½ teaspoons dried oregano

2 tablespoons vegetable oil

1 large yellow onion, diced

2 cups canned white hominy, drained

3 Roma tomatoes, cored, seeded, and diced

4 cups chicken stock

Salt and pepper to taste

Garnishes: 1 cup sliced radishes, shredded lettuce, 1 cup diced onion, 2 cups fried corn tortilla strips or crushed corn chips, 1 cup diced avocado, ¼ cup dried oregano, and 10 lime wedges

1 Combine the chicken, salt, and water in a pot. Bring to a boil, reduce to a simmer, and cook, uncovered, until barely done, about 15 minutes. Let cool and then strain, reserving the broth. Cover the chicken with a wet tea towel and set aside.

2 Soak the chiles in the reserved warm broth for 20 minutes. Add the garlic and oregano, transfer to a blender, and puree until smooth.

3 Heat the oil in a medium stockpot over medium-high heat. Sauté the onion until lightly golden, about 10 minutes. Add the pureed chile mixture, hominy, tomatoes, 4 cups of chicken stock, and chicken. Bring to a boil, reduce to a simmer, and cook, uncovered, until the chicken is tender, about 30 minutes longer. Stir occasionally to prevent the hominy from sticking to the bottom of the pan.

4 Season with salt and pepper and serve in large soup bowls. Bring the garnishes to the table for sprinkling to taste.

To taste the more traditional version of posole, substitute 2½ pounds of trimmed, cubed pork butt for the chicken. For green posole, you can substitute 4 jalapeños for the anchos and 8 tomatillos for the tomatoes. Garnish with cilantro.

One interesting thing we noticed when we opened our first Border Grill was that the produce bill went up 50 percent from our previous restaurant, where we served European-based cuisine. Our produce costs didn't increase because people were ordering more salads. They went up because good Mexican cooking calls for loads of fresh vegetables.

Without a native tradition to fall back on, we gathered inspiration from the Mexican marketplace and combined it with our veteran salad-making skills in creating this selection of Mexican-style salads. As Los Angeles restaurateurs, we are always on the lookout for fresh salad ideas because 40 percent of our lunch guests order salad.

In this chapter, we include the well-loved tostada and Caesar salads, healthful starch-based bean, bread, and quinoa salads for larger appetites, and even a marinated cactus salad for those who are ready to expand their culinary experiences.

Preparing the Greens

Always wash and dry your salad greens. To wash a large quantity of greens, first cut away the cores and stems of the leaves. Then fill a clean sink or large bowl with cold water, add the lettuce leaves, and soak for 10 minutes so that the sand sinks to the bottom. Lift out the leaves, shake off the excess water, and pat the leaves dry with paper towels or spin them dry with a salad spinner.

If you like to have a salad every day like I do, here is a time-saving tip: Wash and dry your lettuce as much as one week in advance. Just slip the well-dried leaves into a plastic bag with a piece of paper towel and store in the vegetable bin of the refrigerator. Also, the pre-washed, bagged salads sold in the supermarket are fine substitutes for the time-pinched home cook.

Dressing the Greens

- Mix your salad in a bowl that's twice as large as what you appear to need. The bigger, the better for carefree tossing.

- Generally, dressings are made with three parts oil to one part vinegar or lemon. But we agree with Mexican cooks who favor a 50/50 split—nice and sour! To our cooking colleagues, we're known as the acid queens!

- The salad fixings (except for the onions which lose their fresh flavor quickly once cut) and dressing can be made in advance and chilled.

- If you make your dressing ahead, store it in a bottle that holds twice the volume of the dressing. Then you can give the bottle a good shake to completely mix it before drizzling it over the vegetables.

- After you place all the ingredients in the bowl, start adding the dressing about 2 tablespoons at a time, tossing and tasting between additions. Less is best to begin with because you can always add but you can't subtract dressing. Your ultimate goal should be to thinly coat each ingredient, without a pool of dressing remaining on the bottom of the bowl.

- The all-time best tool for tossing salad is your hands. Because you can spread your fingers wider than a fork, and your hands are more flexible, you can truly lift and separate the ingredients. So keep 'em clean, dig into that salad bowl, and stir and toss with abandon. It's even okay to take a bite. How else can you tell if the dressing is right?

Before tossing out that leftover salad, place it back in the fridge. Soggy salad is delicious the next day if you mound it on toast and top it with a hot fried egg for breakfast.

The Tostada: A Salad in Disguise

Tostadas are wonderful, healthful salads served on edible fried tortilla plates. With their small meat portions, they make terrific all-in-one suppers. You also can think of them as healthful sandwiches because they combine carbos (corn), veggies, and a little bit of meat.

The key to a terrific tostada is to season each part separately and well. The chicken or meat, as well as the salad, should be moistened and seasoned with dressing so that every bite is moist and flavorful. You almost force people to eat the perfect balance of foods by putting something with acidity and texture on top of something rich like the beans. If you serve salad on the side, people tend to eat it separately.

In a tostada, spread the beans out to all the edges and scatter the other components evenly. Each bite should deliver a combination of flavors. Who wants a mouthful of plain tortilla with those wonderful tastes congregating in the middle?

Chicken Tostada Salad

Preparation time: *25 minutes*

Cooking time: *15 minutes*

Yield: *4 servings (8 tostadas)*

¾ pound cooked, shredded chicken

1 small red onion, diced

1 bunch cilantro leaves, chopped (about ½ cup)

1 small or ½ large head romaine lettuce, finely shredded

1 medium tomato, cored, seeded, and diced

½ cup (2 ounces) grated añejo cheese

½ cup red wine vinegar

¾ cup olive oil

Salt and pepper to taste

¾ cup vegetable oil for frying

8 large (6-inch) corn tortillas or 8 prepared tostada shells

1 cup Refried Black Beans or good-quality canned refried beans

Garnishes: 3 tablespoons Crema and 1 large avocado or 2 medium avocados, peeled, seeded, and thinly sliced

1 Combine the chicken, onion, and cilantro in a medium bowl.

2 In another bowl, combine the lettuce, tomato, and cheese.

3 To make the dressing, combine the red wine vinegar, olive oil, and salt and pepper in a small jar or bottle. Cover and shake vigorously to combine, or whisk the ingredients together.

4 Pour the vegetable oil to a depth of ½ inch in a small frying pan. Heat the oil over moderate heat. Fry the tortillas on both sides until crisp and drain on paper towels.

5 Heat the beans through in a small pot over low heat, stirring often to prevent sticking. Add some water if beans are dry.

6 To assemble, spread a thin layer of beans on each crisp tortilla. Drizzle with about 1 teaspoon Crema and top with a few avocado slices. Pour enough dressing on the reserved chicken mixture to coat generously and toss well. Scatter over the tortillas. Toss the remaining dressing with the lettuce mixture and generously cover each tostada with it.

All-Star Side Salads

Although I know that "salad" means leafy greens for lots of people, I look for salads packed with interesting, contrasting elements and don't worry too much about the lettuce. For example, Mexican Chopped Salad (see the following recipe) has so much going for it— refreshing green apples, salty chips, rich nuts, and fragrant spice—that lettuce never really enters my mind at all.

Mexican Chopped Salad

This unusual chopped salad of tart green apples, corn, and pine nuts is a best-seller at our Santa Monica Border Grill and appeals especially to the advanced salad maker and eater. The broken tortilla chips supply the crunch ordinarily delivered by salad croutons.

Make sure not to get stuck on these particular ingredients. Almonds can stand in for the pine nuts, jícama for the apple—you get the idea. Whatever you have in the house will be perfect.

Preparation time: *20 minutes*

Cooking time: *5 minutes*

Yield: *4 servings*

⅓ cup pine nuts

1 teaspoon ground cumin

Salt and pepper to taste

¼ cup red wine vinegar

½ cup extra-virgin olive oil

1 small or ½ large head romaine lettuce, cut into ½-inch strips

2 medium tomatoes, cored, seeded, and diced

1 small red onion, diced

1 medium green apple, peeled, cored, and diced

½ cup fresh corn kernels (cut from 1 ear of corn)

1½ cups crushed tortilla chips

Garnish: 1 avocado, peeled, seeded, and thinly sliced

1 To make the dressing, toast the pine nuts in a small dry frying pan over medium heat for 2 minutes, shaking frequently. Add the cumin and continue toasting and shaking the pan, 1 minute longer. Remove from heat. Add the salt and pepper, vinegar, and olive oil to the pan and whisk until the ingredients blend. Let cool.

2 In a large bowl, combine the lettuce, tomatoes, onion, apple, corn kernels, and tortilla chips. Toss well. Drizzle with dressing. Toss until well-coated. Top with avocado slices and serve.

Cactus Paddle Salad

Our experience with serving cactus in the restaurant tells us that if you try it, chances are you'll like it—especially if you don't know what you're eating. So stop being a food wimp and let a little cactus into your life! This is our most authentic Mexican salad because cactus is such a popular ingredient there—it's served all over the country.

Preparation time: *20 minutes, plus 2 hours chilling*

Cooking time: *5 minutes*

Yield: *4 to 6 servings*

1½ pounds fresh or prepared cactus paddles, or nopales, needles removed

2 serrano chiles, finely diced

1 bunch cilantro leaves, chopped (½ cup)

¾ cup olive oil (or ½ cup if you're using canned cactus)

½ teaspoon salt

4 Roma tomatoes, cored, seeded, and diced

½ small red onion, diced

½ cup finely grated añejo cheese

¼ cup red wine vinegar

Salt and pepper to taste

4 to 6 red lettuce leaves

Garnish: 1 avocado, peeled, seeded, and thinly sliced

1 Preheat the grill medium hot or heat the broiler.

2 For fresh cactus, place the cleaned paddles in a large bowl and toss with ¼ cup of the olive oil and the ½ teaspoon salt. Grill or broil the paddles until grill marks appear on both sides, or until the paddles turn dark green with black patches, about 4 minutes total. Set aside to cool to room temperature. Cover and chill for at least 2 hours or overnight. If using canned cactus, simply drain well and skip the grilling, omitting the ¼ cup of olive oil used for grilling.

3 Cut the cactus into ½-inch pieces. In a large bowl, combine the cactus, tomatoes, onion, chiles, cilantro, and cheese with the remaining ½ cup oil, vinegar, and salt and pepper. Toss well. Serve on plates lined with lettuce leaves and garnish with avocado slices.

If you can't get cactus, try this salad with sliced grilled chayote or winter squash in place of the cactus.

The miraculous cactus

Since ancient times, the parts of the cactus have served many purposes in Mexican life. Prickly spines were used as fish hooks, needles, and even toothpicks by the Aztecs. Tall, columnar stems are still in use today to construct fences, while green paddles are chopped for animal fodder and munched on by wild animals.

Cactus's curative powers are legendary. Tiny cactus paddles are said to help cure coughs, diabetes, stomach ailments from ulcers to diarrhea and constipation, and inflammation of the molars.

The fruit is used to produce candy, syrups, marmalades, and a brilliant red dye, and the roots of this desert plant also help prevent soil erosion.

Watercress and Radish Salad

The idea for this simple but vibrant combination came from a Mexico City marketplace. That's where we saw radishes ranging from white to pink, purple, and red in a wide variety of shapes displayed right next to bushels of brilliant green watercress—one of our favorite tart greens. We were surprised to learn that watercress is a popular ingredient in Mexico. It's used for green moles, salsas, and garnishes.

Preparation time: *10 minutes*

Yield: *6 servings*

2 bunches red radishes (12 to 15), washed and trimmed

4 bunches watercress, washed and 1-inch stems trimmed

⅓ cup olive oil

3 tablespoons freshly squeezed lime juice

Salt and pepper to taste

1 Thinly slice the radishes into half moons. Combine the radishes and watercress in a large bowl.

2 To make the dressing, in a small bowl whisk together the olive oil, lime juice, and salt and pepper. Pour over the salad and toss well to coat. Serve immediately on chilled plates.

Cracked black pepper is the perfect salad accompaniment. I adore pepper and often use fresh cracked peppercorns moistened with olive oil to sprinkle over a sliced avocado half on my salads. For a fuller-bodied watercress salad, fan avocado slices across the top and give them the cracked pepper treatment.

Watercress is a great little green to work with. Although it often gets overlooked in our rush to embrace the new, it has a similar bite to more expensive greens like arugula and is easy to find. Even the stems are edible. We just trim the woody, bottom part.

Caesar Salad

Are you surprised to see this recipe for Caesar Salad included in a book on Mexican cooking? Although most people associate this salad with Italian cooking, its true origins are in Mexico.

The Caesar salads served in restaurants are often just too rich for our tastes. This one has just the right balance of lime juice and vinegar to the rich combination of egg, salty anchovy, and cheese.

Preparation time: *20 minutes*

Cooking time: *15 minutes*

Yield: *6 servings*

1 egg, refrigerated

3 cloves garlic, crushed and peeled

5 canned anchovy fillets, not rinsed

2 teaspoons Dijon mustard

1 teaspoon celery salt

Salt

½ teaspoon pepper

½ cup extra-virgin olive oil

3 tablespoons red wine vinegar

2 tablespoons lime juice

3 dashes of Tabasco sauce

3 dashes of Worcestershire sauce

3 tablespoons olive oil

½ loaf (8 ounces) sourdough or hearty French or Italian bread, with crust, cut in ¾-inch cubes for large croutons (3 to 4 cups)

2 medium heads romaine lettuce

⅔ cup freshly grated añejo cheese

1 Bring a small saucepan of water to a boil. Place a refrigerated egg on a slotted spoon and gently lower into boiling water. Cook for 1½ minutes, remove, and reserve.

2 To make the dressing, place the garlic and anchovies in a large bowl and mash with a fork until smooth. Add the mustard, celery salt, salt, pepper, ½ cup olive oil, vinegar, lime juice, Tabasco, and Worcestershire sauce. Crack open the egg and, with a spoon, scrape out all the egg, including the uncooked parts, into the bowl. Whisk until well combined. The dressing may be refrigerated at this stage.

3 Heat the 3 tablespoons olive oil in a large cast-iron skillet over medium-low heat. Add the croutons and cook, stirring constantly, until golden and crisp, about 10 minutes.

4 Wash and dry the lettuce and break it into bite-sized pieces. Place in a salad bowl, along with the dressing and grated cheese, and toss well. Add the toasted croutons, toss again, and serve.

TOQUE TIP

Although the egg may still look runny or even completely raw after you cook it, you needn't worry. One minute of cooking time is long enough to kill any bacteria. By cooking the egg for more than a minute, any threat of salmonella has been eliminated. Use this technique in any recipe calling for raw egg if you are concerned with safety.

All hail, Caesar

It's difficult to separate fact from folklore when it comes to tracing the bloodlines of such a popular and idiosyncratic dish as the Caesar salad. However, we do know that the Caesar salad was invented in Mexico during the Prohibition era when Americans would drive over the border for a drink with dinner. The creators, Tijuana restaurateurs Alex and Caesar Cardini, perfected it as a main course with whole lettuce leaves, no anchovies, and two barely-cooked eggs. To enhance its allure, each signature salad was assembled tableside.

We can easily imagine these inventive brothers with a restaurant full of hungry, thirsty visitors from Los Angeles. As they searched for inspiration among the condiments and spices, they eventually created a salad dressing so special that all it needed was some lettuce and croutons to be a complete dish. In Los Angeles, a bottled Caesar salad dressing bearing the Cardini name is still sold in the markets.

Keen on quinoa

It's hard to feel cozy about an ingredient that you can't even pronounce, so we want to get that out of the way right now: KEEN-wah is the way you say it.

Quinoa is a tiny, bead-shaped, cream-colored, plain-tasting grain similar to couscous. When boiled in water, it expands to four times its size.

Quinoa is a complete protein. It's high in unsaturated fats and low in carbohydrates and is a more balanced source of nutrients than any other grain. An added bonus is its ease of preparation. Unlike rice, quinoa is impossible to mess up—it never turns out too watery or gooey or clumpy.

Look for quinoa in your health food store and try to purchase the organic variety. This is one ingredient where the taste of organic makes a big difference.

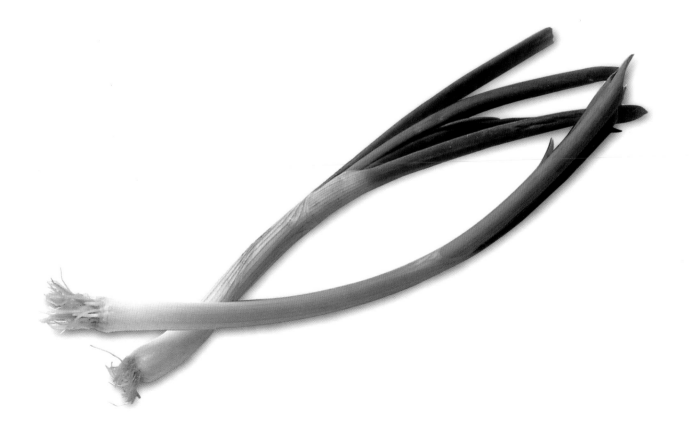

Chapter 5

• • • • • • • • • •

The Essential Sides: Rice, Beans, Tortillas, and Vegetables

In This Chapter

• • • • • • • • • • • • •

▸ Frying rice Mexican-style

▸ Enjoying beans for all seasons

▸ Making tortillas and chips at home

• • • • • • • • • • • • • • •

In these delicious side dishes, salsa, chiles, and herbs bring rice to a whole new level of interest. Beans are mashed and enriched with fat to make luxuriously creamy refried beans. Old tortillas never die or get thrown out; instead, they are reborn as crispy, scrumptious tortilla chips and tostadas.

In addition to their ability to breathe new life into simple ingredients, some of these side dishes are also very healthy. Remember that combining beans (without lard, of course) and rice forms a full protein.

This chapter focuses on the simple, inexpensive side dishes that most Mexican meals are built around. In most Mexican homes, a pot of beans is always bubbling on a burner, there's rice in the fridge for reheating, and tortillas are always present.

Getting the Rice Spirit

The Mexican method for cooking rice is a great example of how the simplest foods can become a special occasion in the hands of gifted cooks. Frying the rice to develop a toasty flavor and then infusing it with salsa to give it color, flavor, and pizzazz is one of the most exciting techniques we've learned from the Mexican kitchen. Although cooking rice the Mexican way takes more time than the ways you may be used to cooking rice, these special rice dishes are well worth the extra effort.

To get the most from your Mexican rice, you need to start with the right ingredients and treat them right during preparation. Follow these tips to increase your success:

- ✔ Start with well-rinsed long-grain rice. We always rinse rice before cooking to remove the excess starch that causes gumminess. To rinse the rice, place it in a large bowl, not a colander, and rinse under cold running water for 5 minutes, or until the water runs clear. Keep stirring the grains with your hand to loosen starch particles.

- ✔ If your recipe calls for you to toast the rice (which is done on the stove top in a skillet, rather than in the oven), go for a full golden color and roasted aroma.

- ✔ Always let your rice rest before serving it. Doing so allows the rice to finish cooking and cool slightly.

- ✔ Stirring rice with a spoon to cool it down can break delicate grains. Instead, use a fork to gently separate the rice and cool it down before serving it. Cool overcooked or mushy rice by emptying it out onto a baking sheet and spreading it thinly so that air can circulate.

    ✔ For an interesting twist, try tossing some broken, dry spaghetti or tiny, whole orzo into the pot along with the rice and fry until golden. If you want to add the spaghetti, use the thin-style spaghetti and break it into small pieces of about ¼ inch.

    ✔ More is always better than less when adding chiles and salsas to these rice dishes. Creating a full-flavored rice takes a gutsy dose of spice and salsa.

White Rice

We like to serve white rice with heavily spiced foods that benefit from something soothing for balance. For example, serve this rice with the Dark Mole with Turkey or Chile Braised Lamb Shanks.

Preparation time: *5 minutes*

Cooking time: *45 minutes*

Yield: *6 to 8 servings*

3 tablespoons vegetable oil

1½ cups long-grain white rice, rinsed

½ medium onion, diced

1 clove garlic, peeled and minced

Salt and pepper to taste

3½ cups chicken stock, vegetable stock, or water

Heat the oil in a medium saucepan over medium-low heat. Sauté the rice and onion, stirring constantly, until a very light golden color, about 5 minutes. Add the garlic and salt and pepper and cook 1 minute longer. Pour in the stock or water and bring to a boil. Reduce to a simmer, cover, and cook for 20 minutes. Add a bit more liquid if longer cooking is necessary. Let rest 10 minutes, fluff with a fork, and serve.

Green Rice

Don't be shy about the amount of greens in this flavorful side dish. Our favorite rice is definitely not the kind to fade into the background. This tomatillo-infused rice makes a great sidekick to Citrus Chicken or Cumin and Chile Marinated Skirt Steak.

Special tool: *Food processor or blender*

Preparation time: *15 minutes*

Cooking time: *45 minutes*

Yield: *6 to 8 servings*

½ cup cold water

2 poblano chiles, roasted, peeled, and seeded

2 romaine lettuce leaves

1 bunch cilantro, stems and leaves, coarsely chopped (½ cup)

2 scallions, white and green parts cut into 1- to 2-inch pieces

2 cloves garlic, peeled

6 tomatillos, coarsely chopped

1 teaspoon salt

1 to 1½ cups chicken stock, vegetable stock, or water

3 tablespoons vegetable oil

1½ cups long-grain rice, rinsed

1 Pour the ½ cup water into a food processor or a blender. Add the chiles, lettuce leaves, cilantro, scallions, garlic, tomatillos, and salt. Puree until liquefied, adding enough stock or water to bring to 3½ cups. (If using a blender, work in batches.) Set aside.

2 Heat the oil in a medium-size heavy saucepan over medium-low heat. Sauté the rice, stirring constantly, until golden and crackling, about 5 minutes. Pour in the reserved green puree and stir to combine. Bring to a boil, reduce to a simmer, cover, and cook until the liquid is absorbed and the rice is tender, about 20 minutes. Let rest 10 minutes. Fluff with a fork and serve hot.

Red Rice

This is the basic tomato-tinged rice that accompanies so many Mexican dishes. You can make the Red Roasted Tomato Salsa, which gives the rice its color, as long as a week in advance. Red Rice is delicious with Cochinita Pibil or Chipotle Glazed Chicken.

Preparation time: _5 minutes, plus 35 minutes for the Red Roasted Tomato Salsa_

Cooking time: _45 minutes_

Yield: _6 to 8 servings_

3 tablespoons vegetable oil

1½ cups long-grain rice, rinsed

½ medium yellow onion, chopped

2 cloves garlic, peeled and chopped

Salt and pepper to taste

5 serrano chiles, or to taste, stemmed, seeded if desired

2 cups chicken stock, vegetable stock, or water

1½ cups Red Roasted Tomato Salsa

_1_ Heat the oil in a medium-size heavy saucepan or skillet over medium-low heat. Sauté the rice, stirring constantly, until golden brown and crackling, about 5 minutes. Add the onion and sauté just until soft. Stir in the garlic, salt and pepper, and chiles and sauté until the aroma is released.

_2_ Pour in the stock or water and the salsa, mixing well to combine. Bring to a boil, reduce to a simmer, cover, and cook for 20 minutes. Let rest 10 minutes. Fluff with a fork and serve hot.

Beautiful, Beautiful Refried Beans!

With their dollop of richness from lard or other fat, refried beans are an inexpensive way to satisfy the universal need to feel full and happy. Refrieds are a little more special than ordinary beans, and they're typically served alongside small snacks like tacos or enchiladas to round out the meal.

In Mexico, small black beans are more popular in the south, while pink pintos are favored in the north. Any kind of bean can be fried in fat and mashed.

Bean dips and nachos are a great way to use leftover refried beans!

In this section, we give you recipes for making refrieds with both black and pinto beans. Regardless of which color you decide to go with, follow these tips as you prepare your beans:

- Wash and pick over your beans before cooking. Wash them in a colander with cold water and then spread the beans out on a cookie sheet or counter. Pull out and discard any stray dirt, stones, or shriveled beans.

- Both of our refried bean recipes ask you to use lard because that is the most typical Mexican fat for beans and it adds a hint of pork flavor that makes the dish delicious. You can't fry beans without fat, but you can use different fats if lard is not to your liking. In place of the lard, you can substitute bacon drippings, vegetable oil, or half butter and half olive oil in the same quantity as specified.

Refried Black Beans

Frying beans with a bit of fat and onion accentuates their rich, creamy quality. Our own tastes tend toward even more lard than the following recipes calls for, but we don't want to scare away the faint-hearted. Remember that if you don't eat refried beans with lots of meat or protein, the overall proportion of fat in the meal is not unhealthy. Serve these fantastic beans with tacos.

Special tool: *Potato masher*

Preparation time: *10 minutes*

Cooking time: *1 hour and 30 minutes*

Yield: *4 to 6 servings*

2 cups dried black beans, washed and picked over

8 cups water

⅓ cup lard or vegetable oil

1 large onion, diced

1½ teaspoons salt

½ teaspoon freshly ground black pepper

1 Place the beans and water in a large pot and bring to a boil. Cover, reduce to a simmer, and cook for 1 hour and 15 minutes, or until the beans are tender and creamy in the center. (To test for doneness, taste 3 or 4 of the smaller beans.) Crush the beans in their liquid with a potato masher or the back of a wooden spoon.

2 Heat the lard or vegetable oil in a large saucepan over medium heat. Sauté the onion with the salt and pepper until golden, about 10 minutes. Add the beans and their liquid and continue cooking over medium heat, stirring frequently, until the liquid evaporates and the beans form a creamy mass that pulls away from the bottom and sides of the pan, about 15 minutes. Serve immediately.

If you are lucky enough to find epazote, a sprig or two added to the pot of the refried beans for the last 15 minutes gives the beans an authentic flavor. Epazote has also been known to counteract the unpleasant side effect of beans on the digestive system!

Refried Pinto Beans

Though black beans are fashionable these days, we still love big, creamy, crushed pintos alongside a bowl of Carnitas Norteñas or Cumin and Chile Marinated Skirt Steak.

Special tool: *Potato masher*

Preparation time: *10 minutes*

Cooking time: *2 hours*

Yield: *4 to 6 servings*

8½ cups water

2 cups dried pinto beans, washed and picked over

½ cup lard or vegetable oil

1 large yellow onion, diced

1 teaspoon salt

½ teaspoon pepper

1 Bring the water to a boil in a medium saucepan. Add the beans, reduce to a simmer, cover, and cook, skimming foam from the top occasionally, approximately 1 hour and 45 minutes. (To test for doneness, taste 3 or 4 of the smaller beans. They should be cooked through and creamy inside.) Mash the beans, along with the liquid in the pot, with a potato masher or the back of a wooden spoon until creamy.

2 Heat the lard or vegetable oil in a medium saucepan over medium-high heat. Sauté the onion with the salt and pepper until golden brown, about 10 minutes. Add the mashed beans and continue cooking, stirring occasionally, until the liquid evaporates and the beans form a mass that pulls away from the sides and bottom of the pan, about 10 minutes. Serve immediately.

 If you prefer your beans boiled, "in the pot" as they are known in Mexico, just skip the mashing and ladle the boiled beans with their liquid into bowls to serve. Sprinkle with diced fresh onion, jalapeño, and cilantro.

Making Your Own Corn Tortillas

Handmade corn tortillas have a pebbly texture and a definitive, earthy corn flavor. They're a wonderful addition to a Mexican-themed party, where their heavenly aroma is sure to draw guests into the kitchen to start the nibbling. In the Mexican home, fresh tortillas are bought daily, as the French buy baguettes.

Corn Tortillas

The Quaker Oats brand of masa harina or the Aztec Milling Company's deep yellow masa harina works well in this recipe.

Special tool: *Tortilla press*

Preparation time: *15 minutes*

Cooking time: *20 minutes*

Yield: *12 to 18 6-inch tortillas*

2 cups masa harina

1 to 1½ cups lukewarm water

Pinch of salt

1 Combine the masa harina and salt in a large mixing bowl and add the lukewarm water while stirring, until smooth. The dough should be slightly sticky and form a ball when pressed together. To test, flatten a small ball of dough between your palms or 2 sheets of plastic wrap. If the edges crack, add more water a little at a time until a test piece does not crack.

2 Divide the dough into 12 to 18 pieces depending upon the size you prefer for your tortillas. Roll each piece into a ball and place the ball on a plate covered with a damp cloth towel.

3 Heat a dry cast-iron or nonstick frying pan or a stovetop griddle over medium heat. Flatten each ball of dough between 2 sheets of heavy plastic wrap either in a tortilla press or on a counter by using your hands or with a rolling pin. Remove the plastic from the top and, holding the tortilla with your fingertips, peel off the bottom sheet of plastic. Lay the tortillas, one by one, on the griddle and cook for about 1 minute and 15 seconds per side, gently pressing the top of the second side with your fingertips to encourage the tortilla to puff. Use tongs or a spatula to turn.

4 Cool the hot tortillas in a single layer on a towel. When they are still warm, but not hot, stack and wrap in the towel. Serve immediately or let cool, wrap well in plastic, and store in the refrigerator up to 1 week. Corn tortillas can be frozen for 2 weeks.

Reheating tortillas

To reheat refrigerated corn or flour tortillas, just follow these steps:

> **1. Heat the oven to 200°.**
>
> **2. Warm a tea towel by placing it on a baking sheet and putting it in the oven briefly.**
>
> **3. Place a dry skillet over medium heat. Warm the tortillas in the skillet, one at a time, about 30 seconds per side, and stack them, covering them with the warm towel between additions.**
>
> If the tortillas are dry, sprinkle them with water before reheating.
>
> **4. Wrap stacked tortillas in the towel, wrap the towel with foil, and place in the oven until ready to serve.**

Frying a corn tortilla (and turning it into a tortilla chip)

Fried whole tortillas serve as the base for tostadas, or you can break up the fried tortilla into chips to be served with all manner of salsas. Strips of fried tortillas are often used as garnishes.

Sure, there are plenty of serviceable tortilla chips on the market, but if you're going to master Mexican cooking at home, you owe it to yourself to experience some homemade chips and taste the difference. A recently fried tortilla chip has so much more character and crispness that it becomes more than a vehicle for other flavors. It's delicious all by itself.

Our homemade corn tortillas are great for chip making because they have less moisture to fry out than bagged tortillas. But, of course, you don't have to start absolutely from scratch. Stale, old tortillas that have been lurking in your refrigerator for longer than you care to remember are ideal for chip making.

Whatever you start with, leave the tortillas out on a counter to dry before frying. Then follow these steps to fry them:

1. For strips, cut the tortilla in half and then thinly slice across the width. For chips, cut in half and cut each half into 4 wedges. For tostadas, keep the tortilla whole.

2. Pour vegetable oil into a large pot or skillet to a depth of about 2 inches. Place over medium-high heat and heat to 375°, or until a piece of tortilla, when dropped in the oil, bubbles and rises to the surface.

3. Fry wedges and strips a handful at a time, stirring with a slotted spoon to separate, until very lightly browned all over. If frying whole tortillas, use tongs to turn.

4. Transfer to paper towels to drain. Sprinkle with salt while warm and serve in bowls for munching. When completely cooled, store in resealable plastic bags or any airtight container at room temperature.

Spicing Things Up with Veggie Sides

We love to eat our veggies. In fact, if we weren't chefs, we just might cross the line and become vegetarians. So many of our customers in Los Angeles want to eat light and healthy that we always take special care with our vegetable dishes so that they're as special as everything else on the menu. These Mexican sides are so rich-tasting and flavorful you'll wonder how you ever settled for steamed vegetables.

Mashed Yams with Sour Cream and Honey

We love to add something sour to sweet yams to offset their candylike quality. If you prefer to avoid the calories of sour cream, feel free to substitute the juice of one lime.

Special tool: *Potato masher*

Preparation time: *15 minutes*

Cooking time: *1 hour and 45 minutes*

Yield: *6 to 8 servings*

6 small or medium yams (about 4 pounds)

3 tablespoons butter, room temperature

½ cup sour cream

Salt and pepper to taste

2 tablespoons honey or to taste (optional)

1 Preheat the oven to 350°.

2 Wash the yams and prick all over with a skewer or fork. Place on a baking tray. Bake until they are soft all the way through and the skins are puffy and oozing, about 1 hour and 30 minutes. Set aside to cool slightly, leaving the oven on.

3 When the yams are cool enough to handle, peel them and place in a medium baking dish. Add the butter, sour cream, and salt and pepper. Stir and mash well with a potato masher. Drizzle the top with honey, if desired, and return to the oven for 15 minutes, until heated through and browned on top. Serve hot.

Avoid cooking with fresh sweet potatoes or yams in June or July. Those still on the market have been in cold storage eight months or more and will be dry, stringy, and sometimes wrinkled from shrinkage.

When I don't have sour cream in the house to dress these potatoes, I mix cream cheese with milk or a little plain yogurt until it's the consistency of pancake batter and use that instead.

Poblano Mashed Potatoes

These spicy, rich potatoes are one of the most frequently requested recipes at our restaurants. Serve with an entrée of equal heft—like a juicy grilled Chile and Garlic Stuffed Rib Eye or Cumin Pepper Lamb Chops.

Special tool: *Potato masher or food mill*

Preparation time: *15 minutes*

Cooking time: *35 minutes*

Yield: *6 servings*

2½ pounds baking potatoes, peeled and quartered

1½ tablespoons salt

1 cup sour cream

½ cup olive oil

5 poblano chiles, roasted, peeled, seeded, and diced

Salt and pepper to taste

1 Place the potatoes in a large saucepan. Pour in enough water to cover and add the 1½ tablespoons salt. Bring to a boil, reduce to a simmer, and cook, uncovered, until soft, about 25 minutes. Drain well, return the potatoes to the pan, and, while still warm, mash with a potato masher or food mill until slightly chunky.

2 In a small pot, combine the sour cream, olive oil, and chiles and warm over low heat just until warm to the touch. Too much heat causes the sour cream to separate.

3 Add the sour cream mixture to the potatoes and gently stir just to combine. Season with salt and pepper and serve immediately.

 The worst thing you can do to these mashed potatoes is overmix them. Gently combine them with the sour cream mixture just until mixed. Overzealous mixing and mashing lead to gummy, starchy potatoes.

Fried Plantains

When ripe plantains are fried, they turn into the most delectable, slightly sweet side dish. We love them for breakfast; in fact, fried plantains served over a bowl of white rice is a very common breakfast item in Mexico. They also go great with Cochinita Pibil and Grilled Red Snapper Tikin-Chik, both dishes from the Yucatán.

Preparation time: *5 minutes*

Cooking time: *10 minutes*

Yield: *6 servings*

3 ripe plantains   *4 tablespoons butter*

1 Peel the plantains and cut into ¼-inch slices on the diagonal.

2 Melt the butter in a large skillet over medium heat. Sauté the plantains until golden brown and soft, about 2 to 3 minutes per side. Serve hot.

Use plantains to make south-of-the-border banana pancakes. Just add a diced ripe plantain to pancake batter and cook on the griddle for a heartier, exotic spin on this traditional American breakfast.

If you're looking for sweet-flavored plantains, they need to be thoroughly ripe, as in totally blackened, before frying.

Seared Chard

This recipe could change the way you think about cooking and eating your greens. After you master this quick searing technique, you'll be able to use it to whip up your favorite leafy greens on a moment's notice—without relying on a recipe.

Chard is a dark green, leafy vegetable with a thick white stem. Vitamin- and mineral-rich spinach, mustard, kale, escarole, dandelion, and turnip greens all taste fabulous cooked this simple, lowfat way. Serve alongside Grilled Turkey Escabeche.

Preparation time: *10 minutes*

Cooking time: *5 minutes*

Yield: *4 servings*

2 bunches green chard	*½ teaspoon salt*
2 tablespoons butter	*Pepper to taste*
2 tablespoons olive oil	

1 Trim and discard the stems of the chard and wash and dry the leaves, including the triangular core between the leaves. Stack the leaves, roll lengthwise into cylinders, and cut across the rolls into 1-inch strips.

2 Melt 1 tablespoon each of the butter and olive oil in a large skillet over medium-high heat until bubbly. Sauté half of the chard with the salt and pepper, stirring and tossing, for less than a minute, until limp. If the chard begins to brown before it wilts, sprinkle in a few drops of water for steam. Transfer to a covered platter and repeat with the remaining chard. (If your skillet is smaller, just cook in several batches.) Serve immediately.

Don't throw out those leftover seared greens! They are delicious the next day dressed with vinegar or lime juice and a touch of olive oil. Eat the greens as a salad or use them as a layer, in place of lettuce, in a grilled chicken, fish, or fried egg sandwich.

Try combining two or three greens, such as escarole, endive, kale, mustard, or spinach, for an interesting layering of flavors.

Spicy Grilled Corn

Here is a refined version of a popular Mexican street snack. Just one bite will leave you wondering how you'll ever go back to plain old buttered corn.

Special tool: _Pastry or barbecue brush_

Preparation time: _15 minutes, plus 10 minutes soaking_

Cooking time: _15 minutes_

Yield: _6 servings_

6 ears fresh sweet corn, in the husk

4 tablespoons butter, softened

Salt and pepper to taste

2 arbol chiles, seeded, stemmed, and coarsely chopped

2 tablespoons chopped fresh cilantro

1 tablespoon freshly squeezed lime juice

_1_ Preheat the grill to medium-hot.

_2_ Carefully remove the corn silks, leaving the husks attached. Soak the ears of corn in their husks in a large bowl or sink of cold water for 10 minutes.

_3_ In a small bowl, mix together the softened butter, salt and pepper, chiles, cilantro, and lime juice until smooth. Set aside.

_4_ Drain the corn well and place each husk-enclosed ear on the hot grill. Cook for about 12 minutes, turning frequently. The corn is steamed when it loses its raw crunch. Remove each cob from the grill and, when cool enough to handle, strip off and discard the husks.

_5_ Brush each cob with the seasoned butter mixture and return to the grill for a minute or two just to heat. Serve immediately.

Chapter 6

· · · · · · · · · · ·

Main Course Meats

The 5th Wave   By Rich Tennant

"The empanadas are coming out a little tough. Someone just requested a piñata bat to open hers with."

In This Chapter

· · · · · · · · · · · · · ·

▶ Traditional park main dishes

▶ Beautiful beef treats

▶ Luscious lamb main courses

· · · · · · · · · · · · · · · · ·

These very traditional main courses all highlight the rich meatiness that only comes from good, fresh pork. We love it slow-roasted in banana leaves in Cochinita Pibil, simmered in its own fat in classic Carnitas Nortenas, and marinated and barbecued to perfection in Baby Back Ribs Adobado. When shopping for pork, look for light pink flesh. The freshest tasting pork is always pale, not blood red.

Cochinita Pibil

In this traditional dish from the Yucatán, meat from baby pigs, or *cochinitas*, is marinated in a blend of achiote paste, citrus juices, and spices, wrapped in fragrant banana leaves, and then buried underground for a long, slow bake. The resulting meat is tender, fragrant, earthy, and unlike anything you've ever tasted—even when roasted in an oven, as ours is here.

Special tool: *Large baking dish*

Preparation time: *15 minutes, plus 4 hours marination*

Cooking time: *3 hours and 10 minutes*

Yield: *8 to 10 servings*

½ cup achiote paste or ⅓ cup annatto seeds	1 teaspoon salt
8 cloves garlic, peeled and chopped	2 teaspoons pepper
½ cup freshly squeezed orange juice	4 pounds pork butt, cut in 3-inch cubes
¼ cup freshly squeezed grapefruit juice	2 medium white onions, sliced ½-inch thick
⅓ cup freshly squeezed lime juice	5 Roma tomatoes, sliced ½-inch thick
8 dried bay leaves	1 pound banana leaves, softened over a low flame, or collard greens, stems trimmed and blanched
2 teaspoons cumin seeds	
½ teaspoon ground cinnamon	4 Anaheim chiles, roasted, peeled, and sliced into strips
1 teaspoon dried oregano	
	Pickled Onions for garnish (see following recipe)

1 In a medium bowl, mash together the achiote paste, garlic, orange juice, grapefruit juice, lime juice, bay leaves, cumin seeds, cinnamon, oregano, salt, and pepper with a fork. Add the pork, toss to evenly coat, and marinate in the refrigerator for at least 4 hours.

2 Preheat the oven to 300°.

3 Heat a dry cast-iron skillet over high heat. Char the onion slices until blackened on both sides. Then char the tomato slices on both sides. Reserve.

4 Line a large baking dish with one layer of the banana leaves or collards. Arrange the pork in an even layer and top with the charred onions, tomatoes, chiles, and all the marinade. Cover with banana leaves and wrap the dish tightly in foil.

5 Bake for about 3 hours or until the pork is tender and moist. Remove from the oven and let sit 10 minutes. Unwrap and serve with Pickled Onions, Fried Plantains, and White Rice.

Chicken or lamb, cut in big chunks with the bone in, are both delicious when slow-roasted in the same manner as Cochinita Pibil. Slow roasting chicken or lamb in this way will certainly spark up your family's perception of these meats!

Pickled Onions

These pungent purple onion rings are the natural accompaniment to achiote-seasoned foods from the Yucatán. They're also a good condiment for turkey, barbecued beef, or Pork Torta.

1 red onion, sliced into thin rings

1 teaspoon salt

½ teaspoon dried oregano

1 habañero chile, seeded and sliced

½ cup freshly squeezed orange juice

¼ cup freshly squeezed lime juice

1 Place the onion rings in a bowl and pour on enough boiling water to cover them. Let sit for 2 minutes. Drain, add the salt, oregano, chile, orange juice, and lime juice, and store in the refrigerator for 4 hours or as long as 2 days.

Baby Back Ribs Adobado

Ribs need special attention to cook up tender, juicy, and falling off the bone. We like to first give ours a strong spice rub for flavor, followed by a steamy bake for tenderness, and then a quick turn on the grill or in a high oven for a crisp edge and some smoke.

Because undercooked ribs are so awful, steaming a little longer can never hurt.

Preparation time: *20 minutes, plus 2 hours refrigeration, plus 1 hour and 25 minutes to make the Adobado*

Cooking time: *1 hour and 35 minutes*

Yield: *4 servings*

¼ cup paprika	*2 tablespoons salt*
¼ cup ground ancho chiles or chili powder	*4½ pounds pork baby back ribs*
¼ cup cumin	*3 cups Adobado (see following recipe)*

1 Combine the paprika, chiles, cumin, and salt in a small bowl. Pat the spice mixture all over the ribs. Place in a pan, cover with plastic wrap, and refrigerate for at least 2 hours or overnight.

2 Preheat the oven to 350°.

3 Place the ribs in a single layer in a baking pan and pour in water to a depth of about ¾ inch. Bake, uncovered, for 45 minutes. Cover with foil and return to the oven for an additional 30 minutes.

4 Meanwhile, make the Adobado.

5 Turn up the oven heat to 450° or heat the grill to medium-high.

6 If finishing the ribs in the oven, brush generously with the Adobado and bake for another 10 minutes per side, basting every 5 minutes To grill, generously glaze the ribs and grill for 5 minutes per side, frequently brushing with additional Adobado sauce. Cut the ribs apart and serve hot.

Inexpensive country-style ribs, available at the supermarket, are a meaty, tasty alternative to baby back ribs. After applying the spice rub, steam in a sealed heavy-duty plastic bag in the top of a double boiler over simmering water for 45 minutes. Then finish in a hot oven as described in Step 6.

Adobado

Adobado is a very traditional, sweet, tart Mexican barbecue sauce. It's great to have on hand for heating up with leftover bits of chicken, pork, or lamb and serving on rolls for delicious barbecue sandwiches.

Special tool: *Blender or food processor*

Preparation time: *20 minutes*

Cooking time: *65 minutes*

Yield: *3 cups*

6 ancho chiles, wiped clean	*2 cups chicken stock*
¼ cup white vinegar	*1 tablespoon brown sugar*
1 cup water	*2 tablespoons freshly squeezed orange juice*
2 tablespoons olive oil	*2 tablespoons freshly squeezed lemon juice*
1 medium yellow onion, thinly sliced	*1 tablespoon tomato paste*
3 garlic cloves, peeled and sliced	*½ tablespoon salt*
½ tablespoon ground cumin	*⅛ teaspoon pepper*

1 Briefly toast the chiles directly over a medium gas flame or in a cast-iron skillet until soft and brown, turning frequently to avoid scorching. Transfer the toasted chiles to a saucepan and add the vinegar and water. Bring to a boil, reduce to a simmer, and cook for 10 minutes to soften.

2 Transfer the chiles and liquid to a blender or food processor. Puree until a smooth paste the consistency of barbecue sauce or ketchup is formed, adding 1 or 2 tablespoons of water if necessary to thin. Set aside.

3 Heat the olive oil in a medium saucepan over medium-high heat. Sauté the onion until golden brown, about 10 minutes. Stir in the garlic and cook briefly just to release the aroma. Then stir in the cumin and cook for another minute. Add the chicken stock and reserved chile paste. Bring to a boil, reduce to a simmer, and cook for 20 minutes.

4 Meanwhile, mix together the brown sugar, orange juice, lemon juice, tomato paste, salt, and pepper to form a paste. Add to the simmering stock mixture and cook for 15 minutes longer. Adobado can be stored in the refrigerator for 1 week or frozen indefinitely.

Carnitas Norteñas

Pork chunks slowly simmered in fat develop a heightened pork flavor and silky, smooth texture. Carnitas are delicious in tacos or burritos, with spicy salsa and the Pickled Onions described earlier in this chapter to offset their essential richness.

Preparation time: *10 minutes*

Cooking time: *1 hour and 40 minutes*

Yield: *6 servings*

2 pounds pork shoulder or butt, cut into 2-inch cubes

Salt and pepper to taste

1½ pounds lard or pork fat or shortening

1 medium red onion, freshly diced

1 bunch cilantro, chopped (½ cup)

5 serrano chiles, chopped

Mashed avocado

Warm Corn Tortillas

Green Tomatillo Salsa

1 Generously season the pork all over with salt and pepper.

2 Melt the lard in a large, deep saucepan or Dutch oven over moderate heat. Add the well-seasoned meat and simmer, uncovered, over medium-low heat for 1 hour and 15 minutes, until fork tender. Remove the pork with a slotted spoon and transfer to a cutting board. The fat can be refrigerated for future use.

3 Preheat oven to 400°.

4 When cool enough to handle, shred the pork by hand or with the tines of two forks. In a mixing bowl, toss the pork with the onion, cilantro, and chiles to combine. Transfer to a casserole, cover tightly, and bake, until heated through, about 15 minutes. Serve hot with the mashed avocado, corn tortillas, and Green Tomatillo Salsa.

Beefing Up Your Meals

There's nothing like a properly grilled, well-marbled piece of beef for pleasing guests at a summer barbecue. In Los Angeles, the fragrance of Mexican spices and beef wafting from barbecues is as familiar as the scent of hot dogs at a baseball game.

Tough cuts of beef, like skirt and flank, should always be thinly sliced, across the grain, so that no one bite contains too much chewy muscle.

Cumin and Chile Marinated Skirt Steak

This marinated skirt steak is so flavorful that all it needs is some rice and beans and maybe the Corn and Pepper Compote for contrast.

Special tool: *Blender*

Preparation time: *20 minutes, plus 4 hours marination*

Cooking time: *15 minutes*

Yield: *6 servings*

⅓ cup cumin seeds

6 serrano chiles, stemmed, cut in half, and seeded, if desired

6 cloves garlic, peeled

½ cup freshly squeezed lime juice

2 bunches cilantro, including stems and leaves (1 cup)

½ cup olive oil

Salt and pepper to taste

3 pounds skirt steak, trimmed of excess fat and cut into 6 serving pieces

1 Lightly toast the cumin seeds in a dry medium skillet over low heat just until their aroma is released, about 5 minutes. Transfer the seeds to a blender.

2 Add the serranos, garlic, and lime juice and puree until the cumin seeds are finely ground. Then add the cilantro, olive oil, and salt and pepper and puree until smooth.

3 Generously sprinkle the steak all over with salt and pepper. Generously brush all over with the cumin seed marinade and roll each piece up into a cylinder. Arrange the rolled steaks in a shallow pan and pour on the remaining marinade. Cover and marinate in the refrigerator for at least 4 hours or as long as a day.

4 About 30 minutes before cooking, remove the meat from the refrigerator. Unroll the steaks and place on a platter.

5 Preheat the grill or broiler to very hot.

6 Cook the steaks just until seared on both sides, about 4 minutes per side for medium rare. (Or pan-fry in a hot cast-iron skillet lightly coated with oil.) Transfer to a cutting board and slice across the grain into diagonal strips. Serve hot with warm flour tortillas.

Chile and Garlic Stuffed Rib Eye Steaks

A big, fat, juicy rib eye stands up to strong flavors like chile and garlic. In this easy, spicy steak, those flavors permeate the meat so distinctively that a salsa is not necessary.

Preparation time: *15 minutes*

Cooking time: *20 minutes*

Yield: *4 servings*

¼ cup olive oil

10 jalapeño chiles, stemmed, halved lengthwise, and seeded

20 cloves garlic, peeled

4 rib eye steaks, 10 to 12 ounces each and at least 1-inch thick

Salt and pepper to taste

Garnish: Lime wedges

1 If grilling, preheat the grill to medium-high.

2 Heat the olive oil in a small saucepan over moderate heat. Add the chiles and cook until the skins start to blacken and the chiles soften, about 2 minutes. Remove with a slotted spoon and drain on paper towels. Reduce the heat to low. Add the garlic and cook until soft and lightly browned, about 5 minutes. Transfer to paper towels and let cool.

3 With a paring knife, make 7 to 10 1-inch horizontal slits along the edge of each steak. Stuff each slit with either a garlic clove or chile half. Generously season all over with salt and pepper.

4 Grill the steaks or sauté them in a lightly oiled cast-iron pan over high heat, about 4 minutes per side for medium rare. Serve with lime wedges.

For those who prefer their garlic and chiles on the subtle side, simply remove them before serving. The meat will still have the flavor of heat and spice without any large bites of chili or garlic to upset sensitive palates. And for garlic lovers who are not chile fans, just eliminate the chiles for a wonderfully easy garlic steak.

On the Lamb

Though Americans tend to think of lamb as a special occasion meat, in Mexico it is eaten frequently, along with similar-tasting goat.

Cumin Pepper Lamb Chops with Sweet and Sour Salsa

Thick lamb chops are coated with a crunchy peppercorn and cumin seed crust, similar to the French steak au poivre, and then served with a smooth, tangy salsa. We like a side of potatoes or rice with such an assertive entrée, but for a lighter summer menu, serve these chops over a dressed green salad.

Special tools: *Potato masher, strainer, large cast-iron skillet, large baking dish*

Preparation time: *20 minutes*

Cooking time: *60 minutes*

Yield: *4 servings*

8 ounces tamarind pods, peeled	*½ teaspoon cayenne pepper*
1 tablespoon butter	*1½ tablespoons honey*
3 large garlic cloves, peeled and minced	*¼ cup cracked black pepper*
1 teaspoon salt plus salt to taste	*½ cup cumin seeds*
½ teaspoon ground pepper	*Salt to taste*
½ cup chicken stock	*8 lamb chops, 4 ounces each*
1 tablespoon Worcestershire sauce	*¾ cup vegetable oil*

1 To make the salsa, place the tamarind in a large saucepan and pour in enough water to cover by 1 inch. Cook over medium-low heat, covered, until soft, about 30 minutes. Mash with a potato masher and then push through a strainer, discarding the seeds and strings. Reserve the pulp.

2 Melt the butter in a saucepan over medium-high heat. Sauté the garlic with the salt and pepper until golden brown. Add the mashed tamarind and chicken stock. Bring to a boil, reduce to a simmer, and cook for 10 minutes. Stir in the Worcestershire sauce, cayenne, and honey. Remove from heat and keep warm.

3 Preheat the oven to 350°.

4 Mix together the cracked pepper and cumin seeds in a small shallow bowl. Season the chops all over with salt. Firmly press each into the seed mixture to coat all over. Set aside.

5 In a large skillet, preferably cast-iron, that comfortably holds all 8 chops, heat the oil to very hot, but not smoking. Cook the chops in the bubbling oil until the seeds are golden, about 2 minutes per side. (Do not worry about a few seeds slipping off the chops.) Transfer to a baking dish and bake for 2 minutes for medium rare.

6 To serve, coat 4 plates with the salsa. Top each with 2 lamb chops and serve.

TOQUE TIP To eliminate the unpleasant taste of uncooked lamb fat when cooking chops, use your tongs to stand the meat upright and sear the fat along the edges in the hot pan.

VARIATION If you can't find tamarind, substitute a puree of 2 peeled Granny Smith apples and ½ cup seedless prunes and follow the same cooking times. The result will be a slightly sweeter salsa than with the tamarind.

Appendix

• • • • • • • • • •

More Fun and Treats

• • • • • • • • • • • • • • • • • •
▸ Tantalizing guests and family members with tortilla treats
▸ Creating crunchy snacks with chips
▸ Speaking the language when dining out
▸ Some phrases for shopping in Spanish-speaking countries
• • • • • • • • • • • • • • • • • •

Crisped Tortilla Crackers

Flour tortillas, baked until crisp with different flavorings, make excellent low-cost hors d'oeuvres. Just follow these steps to create this quick and delicious snack:

1. Brush one side of the tortillas with lime juice and sprinkle with ground Chili Powder Mix. Or brush with beaten egg and sprinkle with assorted seeds like sesame, poppy, and flax.

Seeds are available at health food stores.

2. Lay the tortillas, brushed side up, on baking sheets and bake in a 350° oven until crisp, about 8 minutes.

3. Serve in baskets while the crackers are still warm.

For cylindrical crackers, trim ½-inch off each tortilla to create a straight edge. Wrap the tortillas around soda or soup cans and bake until crisp. Then remove the cans and stand the tortillas upright on the table for a dramatic effect.

Tortilla Buñuelos

Make instant *buñuelos,* or fried dough fritters, by deep-frying flour tortillas in oil. Dip the fried tortillas into cinnamon sugar to generously coat, and serve them hot and drizzled with honey for dessert.

The Instant Fish Wrapper

One of our favorite methods for imparting a Mexican flavor to fish fillets is to wrap and bake them in corn tortillas. The tortillas protect the fish and keep it moist while adding a layer of corn flavor.

This fish wrapper works with every sort of fish fillet except tuna or swordfish. Just follow these steps:

1. Marinate the fish fillets in orange and lime juices seasoned with salt, pepper, and oregano for about 1 hour.

2. Briefly saute the fillets until they are halfway cooked. Let cool.

3. Soften the tortillas by dipping them in hot oil, just as you do when making enchiladas. Wrap each fillet in a tortilla or in a triangle made of three overlapping tortillas for larger pieces. Fold over to enclose and wrap in aluminum foil to seal.

4. Bake in a 350° oven until the fish is just done, about 10 minutes.

Chips and Their Crunch

Crushed tortilla chips are a great way to add crunch to salads. Just crunch 'em and toss 'em. Chips can also stand in as crunchy toppings for casseroles.

Add a Mexican touch to your favorite fried or baked foods by using ground or crushed tortilla chips in place of bread crumbs as the coating medium.

Matzoh Brei Mexicana

How's this for cross-cultural chutzpah? Try the Mexican version of matzoh brei, which is the Jewish Passover dish of softened matzoh dipped in egg and scrambled in butter. Just follow these steps:

1. Take 8 ounces of tortilla chips (about 3 large handfuls) and cover them with boiling water to soften. Drain.

In a traditional recipe for matzoh brei, this step would be done with matzoh.

2. Beat the chips together with 3 eggs, salt, pepper, and a chopped serrano or jalapeño chile.

3. Scramble the egg mixture in lots of butter until the edges are brown. Serve hot with sliced scallions, salsa, and sour cream.

Finger Food Wraps

You can use flour tortillas instead of lavosh (the Middle Eastern flat bread) to make pinwheel sandwiches for parties. Just follow these steps:

1. Spread the tortillas with a generous layer of cream cheese.

2. Layer watercress, roasted red and green pepper strips, and thinly sliced salami onto the cream cheese.

3. Roll the tortillas into a cylinder and cut across the width into ½-inch slices. Arrange on platters, cut side up.

Instant Soup Fixins

Crushed tortilla chips or homemade fried corn tortilla strips make excellent crunchy soup garnishes in place of crackers.

Tortilla Ice Cream Sundaes

You can make an instant ice cream topping with flour tortillas by following these steps:

1. Roll a few tortillas into a tight cylinder and thinly slice across the width.

2. Toss the tortillas with melted butter, sugar, and cinnamon and arrange on a baking sheet. Bake at 350° until golden brown.

3. Sprinkle the tortillas over your favorite ice cream—hot fudge sauce is optional.

Roasted, salted peanuts or pecans, by the way, are also very Mexican ice cream toppers.

Healthful Tortilla Stock

You can use tortilla chips as a base for a soulful vegetarian stock for soups and chowders. Just follow these steps:

1. In a soup pot, sauté a coarsely chopped carrot, celery stalk, and onion in 1 tablespoon of oil. When soft, add 1½ quarts of crushed tortilla chips and briefly sauté.

2. Pour in 4 quarts of water, bring to a boil, reduce to a simmer, and cook, uncovered, about 45 minutes, until the flavor has developed.

3. Pass through a strainer, discarding the solids, and store in the refrigerator for 1 week or in the freezer as long as a month.

Chex Mex

Add a Mexican flair to a sweet and salty bar mix by following these steps:

1. Combine diced corn tortillas with peanuts, pepitas, golden raisins, and broken pretzel sticks.

2. Season with peanut oil, Worcestershire sauce, chile powder mix, cayenne, salt, pepper, and a pinch of sugar.

3. Spread on a baking sheet and bake in a 350° oven, stirring occasionally, until crisp, about 10 minutes. Cool before serving.

Ten Spanish Phrases for Travelers

Few things are more frustrating than wanting something in a restaurant or market and not having the words to ask for it. Although we're never too proud to point and act silly in order to get what we want, we've found it makes a big difference if we can at least speak a few words to let people know that we have respect for their culture and we're trying to learn. This way, when the waiter answers our kitchen Spanish in perfect English, we can grin sheepishly, say "Gracias," and humbly enjoy the meal.

Por favor

There's nothing like it. **Por fa-BOR** or "please" is definitely the magic word in any language when it comes to food service. Try to imagine taking orders all day long and never being addressed politely. Simply tack the phrase onto the end of your request and watch your waitperson smile (or at least bring you your food).

Muchas gracias

The partner to "por favor" is **GRAH-see-ahs** or "thank you." If you want to show extreme gratitude, you can add a **MOO-chahs** to the front of it for "thanks so much." You can never say this phrase too much, but do be careful not to mispronounce the gracias. "Grasa" means fat.

Lo quiero mas o menos picante

If you want to give the waitperson a better idea of your tastes, this little phrase should come in handy. **Loh kye-ER-oh mahs** means "I want it more" and **Loh key-ER-oh MEH-nohs** means "I want it less." **Pee-CAHN-teh** means "spicy." So if your heartburn is kicking in, go for option two and, if you're looking for a wilder ride, go for option one.

La cuenta, por favor

We know it's a bittersweet moment, but eventually we all want to get the check and hit the road. **La KWEN-TAH, por fa-BOR,** or "Bring me the bill please" should do the trick.

¿Dónde está el baño?

This is a handy little phrase to have when you're on the road sightseeing and drinking lots of water. **DON-deh es-TAH el BAH-nyo** simply means "Where is the bathroom?"

Quiero ordenar una comida tipica de la region, no la comida de los gringos

No question, this is a mouthful, but you can pick and choose the parts of it that work best for you. **Key-ER-oh or-deh-NAR una koh-MEE-thah TEE-pee-kah deh la re-hyon** means "I want to order a typical dish of the region," and **no la koh-MEE-thah deh los GREEN-gohs** means "not the food the gringos eat." This is the sentence to use if you've waited all your life to taste fried grasshoppers and the waiter is insisting that you'd be better off with a quesadilla. Set him straight and brace yourself for the real thing.

Sin hielo

A practical phrase you should commit to memory before stepping off the plane. **Seen YEH-loh** means without ice, the way you want your drinks in Mexico if you're concerned with traveler's diarrhea. Because it's bacteria in the water that causes the problem, you want to avoid iced drinks. However, some places with a lot of tourist traffic use purified water for ice. If you can string the words together, you can ask about the water in the ice.

Quiero agua purificada

Along with ordering your drinks without ice, another way to ensure you don't spend too much time in your hotel room is by saying **key-ER-oh AH-gwah pu-rih-fi-KAH-dah,** or "I want purified water."

¿Que platillo sugieres?

Keh plah-TEE-yoh suh-hye-RES is a phrase we use when we're not sure what we want to eat but we don't want to miss the specialties of the house. It means "What do you suggest?" or "What dish do you recommend?" and we generally hold the menu up for the waiter to kindly point to. Any waiter worth his or her salt should be happy to offer an opinion.

¿Cuánto cuesta?

We love tasting foods from markets or street vendors who may not have a printed menu. **KWAHN-toh KWEHS-tah,** or "How much is it?" is all you need to know to pay the tab. If you never got past 10 on *Sesame Street,* it's a good idea to carry a pad and pencil for salespeople to write down numbers.

Glossary of Spanish Terms

A

achiote (ah-chee-OH-teh): The seed of annatto tree commonly used for making achiote paste, a seasoning mixture from the Yucatán.

adobado (ah-doh-BAH-doh) or adobo (ah-DOH-boh): A sweet, tart Mexican barbecue sauce or seasoning paste.

agave (uh-GAH-vee): The succulent used for making tequila.

agua fresca (AH-gwah fres-kah): A non-alcoholic fruit juice or tea.

ajo, al mojo de ajo (AH-hoh, ahl-moh-HOH deh AH-hoh): Garlic; a sauce or marinade whose main ingredient is garlic.

ancho (AHN-choh): The dried form of the poblano chile.

añejo (ah-NYEH-hoh): An aged food stuff. Most typically associated with a type of tequila and a Mexican cheese.

arbol (AHR-bohl): A type of paper-thin dried red chile.

arroz con pollo (ah-RROS kohn POH-yoh): A dish of rice with chicken.

atole (ah-TOH-leh): A traditional drink made of corn meal.

B

banda (BAHN-dah): A Mexican band specializing in polka music.

blanco (BLAHN-koh): White; often refers to a clear and unaged type of tequila.

bollillo (boh-LEE-yoh): A plain, crisp white bread roll used for making tortas.

brazo de reina (BRAH-soh deh ray-NAH): A special, large tamale called "the queen's arm."

buñeulo (boo-nyoo-WEH-loh): Sweetened fried dough fritters served for dessert.

burrito (boo-RREE-toh): A snack food of beans, rice, and other fillings wrapped inside a flour tortilla and eaten out of hand.

burro (BUH-roh): A donkey.

C

cabrito (kah-BREE-toh): A young goat; also known in cooked form as birria.

cacao (kah-KAH-oh): Cocoa.

café del olla (kah-FEH del OH-yah): Mexican spiced coffee.

cajeta (kah-HEH-tah): Caramel sauce.

caldo (KAHL-doh): Broth.

caldo de pescado (KAHL-doh deh pehs-KAH-thoh): Fish broth.

caldo de pollo (KAHL-doh deh POH-yoh): Chicken broth.

canela (kah-NEH-lah): Cinnamon.

capirotada (kah-pee-ROH-tah-thah): Mexican bread pudding.

carne asada (KAHR-neh ah-SAH-thah): Roasted or grilled meat, usually skirt steak.

carnitas (kahr-NEE-tahs): A dish of pork chunks simmered in lard.

carnitas norteñas (kahr-NEE-tahs nohr-TEH-nyahs): Northern-style carnitas.

Cascabel (kahs-kah-BEL): A small, dark red, round smooth dried chile.

cerveza (sehr-BEH-sah): Beer.

ceviche (seh-VEE-cheh): A dish of small bits of fish and vegetables marinated in lime juice.

chayote (chah-YOH-the): A small, pale green, wrinkled squash common in Mexico.

chilaca chile (CHEE-lah-kah): A long, thin, dark brown fresh chile.

Chilaquiles (chee-lah-KEE-lehs): A dish made of day-old tortillas and salsa.

chile negro (CHEE-leh NEH-groh): A long, narrow, dark brown dried chile used for grinding into moles.

chiles rellenos (CHEE-lehs reh-YEH-nohs): A dish made of whole chiles that are stuffed and fried.

Chinaco Anejo (chee-NAH-koh ah-NYEH-hoh): A brand of aged tequila.

chipotle (chee-POT-tleh): A smoked and dried jalapeno chile.

chipotle in adobo (chee-POT-leh in ah-DOH-BOH): Canned chipotle chiles in a sweet and sour sauce.

chorizo (choh-REE-soh): Spicy sausage.

churros (CHEW-rrohs): A Mexican pastry of fried dough sprinkled with cinnamon and sugar, often sold on the street.

cochineal (KOH-cheh-neel): An insect used for red dye.

cochinita pibil (koh-chee-NEE-tah pee-BEEL): A dish of small pig cooked in a pit barbecue.

Comal (ko-MAHL): A cast-iron griddle used for making tortillas.

Comino (koh-MEE-noh): The spice cumin.

cotija (koh-TEE-jah): A type of Mexican cheese.

crema (KREH-mah): Mexican sour cream, similar to crème fraiche.

E

El Tresoro Añejo (el treh-SOH-roh ah-NYEH-hoh): A brand of aged tequila.

empanada (em-pah-NAH-thah): A filled pastry similar to a turnover.

Encantado (en-kahn-TAH-thoh): A premium brand of mezcal.

enchilada (en-chee-LAH-thah): A dish of tortillas coated with chili sauce, stuffed and rolled.

enfrijolada (en-free-hoh-LAH-thah): A dish of tortillas dipped in bean sauce.

enmolada (en-moh-LAH-thah): A dish of tortillas dipped in mole sauce.

epazote (eh-pah-SOH-teh): A wild herb used to flavor Mexican dishes .

escabeche (ehs-kah-BEH-cheh): A sweet and sour marinade.

F

fideo (fee-DEH-oh): Angel hair pasta.

fiesta (fee-ES-tah): A celebration.

flan (flahn): A traditional vanilla custard.

Fuerte (FWEAR-teh): A type of avocado.

G

gazpacho (gas-PAH-choh): A typical Spanish style cold tomato soup with vegetables.

guacamole (gwah-kah-MOH-leh): A mashed avocado dip.

Guanajuato (gwan-ah-hwah-toh): A state in central Mexico.

gusano (goo-SAH-noh): The caterpillar often found in a mezcal bottle.

H

habañero (ah-bah-NEH-roh): A type of fresh chile.

horchata (or-CHAH-tah): A drink made from ground rice.

huevos rancheros (WEH-vohs rahn-CHEH-rohs): A dish made of eggs, refried beans, tortillas, and salsa.

J

jalapeño (hah-lah-PEH-nyoh): A type of fresh red or green chile.

Jalisco (hah-LEE-skoh): The Mexican state along the Pacific coast west of Mexico City.

jamaica (hah-MY-kah): Tea brewed from dried hibiscus blossoms.

jícama (HEE-kah-mah): A tuber eaten like a fruit, with crisp white flesh and thick brown skin.

Joven Abocado (HOH-vehn ah-boh-CAH-doh): Gold tequila which is unaged, colored, and sweetened.

L

limón (lee-MOHN): Lemon.

liquados (lee-KWAH-dohs): A fruit shake made with milk or water.

M

magueros (mah-GWEH-rohs): The workers who gather maguey.

maguey (mah-GWEH): The succulent from which mezcal tequila is made, also known as agave.

maiz (mah-EES): Corn.

mañana (mah-NYAH-nah): Morning or tomorrow.

Manchego (mahn-CHEH-goh): A type of Mexican cheese.

manzanillas (mahn-sah-NEE-yahs): Small green Spanish olives.

margarita (mahr-gah-REE-tah): A cocktail consisting of tequila, orange liqueur, and lime or lemon juice.

mariachis (mahr-ee-AH-chees): Mexican band and music, typical of Guadalajara.

masa (MAH-sah): Corn dough.

masa harina (MAH-sah ah-REE-nah): Powdered, dried masa for making tortillas.

masa para tamales (MAH-sah PAH-rah tah-MAH-lehs): Dough made out of dried corn that has been cooked with limestone and water and then coarsely ground for tamales.

menudo (meh-NOO-thoh): A traditional stew of tripe, chiles, and hominy.

mesa (MEH-sah): Table.

metate (meh-TAH-teh): Flat stone used for grinding corn and chiles.

mezcal (mehs-KAHL): A type of tequila from Southern Mexico.

mixto (MEES-toh): A type of tequila made with 60 percent blue agave and 40 percent grain alcohol.

molcajete (mohl-kah-HEH-teh): Mortar of basalt used to grind spices and ingredients.

mole (MOH-leh): A traditional stew made of ground roasted chiles, seeds, and nuts.

mole colorado (MOH-leh koh-loh-RAH-thoh): A reddish-brown mole.

mole poblano (MOH-leh poh-BLAH-noh): A mole from the city of Puebla in central Mexico.

mole verde (MOH-leh BEHR-theh): A green, herb-based mole.

molinillo (moh-LEE-nee-yoh): A traditional wooden whisk for blending hot chocolate.

molino (moh-LEE-noh): Local tradesperson who grinds ingredients for seasonings, moles, and cacao.

mollettes (moh-LEH-tehs): A sandwich made of toasted bread with beans.

morita (moh-REE-tah): A small brown dried chile.

N

naranja agria (nah-RAGHN-hah AH-gree-ah): A bitter orange from Yucatán.

nopale (noh-PAHL): A cactus paddle.

nopalitos (noh-pahl-EE-tohs): Small, young cactus paddles.

p

palapas (pah-LAH-pahs): Beach shacks.

palenque (pah-LEHN-keh): Mezcal distilleries.

pan de yema (pahn deh YEH-mah): An egg-based bread traditionally served on the Day of the Dead and decorated with skull and crossbones.

panela (pah-NEH-lah): A type of fresh white Mexican cheese, similar to Mozzarella.

pasilla (pah-SEE-yah): The dried form of the chilaca chile.

Patrón Añejo (pah-TROHN ah-NYEH-hoh): A brand of aged tequila.

pepita (peh-PEE-tah): A pumpkin seed.

picadillo (pee-kah-DEE-yoh): Seasoned, ground, fried meat, often used for stuffing.

picholines (pee-choh-LEENS): Large, green French olives.

pico de gallo (PEE-koh deh GAH-yoh): A salsa made of chopped fresh tomato.

pina (PEE-nah): The heart of the agave, or maguey plant, used to make tequila.

piñata (peen-YAH-tah): A hanging hollow paper decoration filled with candy and gifts to be broken in a game by blindfolded participants.

pipiáns (pee-PYAHNS): A sauce of ground nuts or seeds and spices, similar to mole.

Plata (PLAH-tah): A type of tequila which is unaged and clear.

poblano (poh-BLAH-noh): A type of fresh green chile used for rajas and stuffing.

Porfidio Silver (pohr-FEE-dee-oh SIL-vehr): A brand of aged tequila.

posole (poh-SOH-leh): A traditional stew of meat and hominy served with several vegetable and herb garnishes.

Puebla (PWEH-blah): City in Central Mexico.

Q

quesadilla (keh-sah-DEE-yah): A flour tortilla with melted cheese filling.

queso fresco (KEH-soh FREHS-koh): A type of fresh white Mexican cheese.

queso fundido (KEH-soh fuhn-DEE-doh): A dish made of melted cheeses and chiles.

quinoa (Aztecan quinoa) (KEEN-wah): A high-protein grain from South America.

R

raja (RAH-hah): A roasted chile strip.

ranchero (rahn-CHEH-roh): Country-style.

Reposado (reh-poh-SAH-thoh): A type of tequila that is aged and light gold in color.

rompope (rohm-POH-peh): Traditional eggnog, usually served at Christmas time.

S

salsa cruda (SAHL-sah CREW-dah): A chopped fresh tomato salsa; also known as pico de gallo.

salsa fresca (SAHL-sah FREHS-kah): Fresh salsa.

salsa verde (SAHL-sah BEHR-theh): A green salsa usually made with tomatillos.

salud (sah-LEWD): A popular toast meaning "to your health."

sandia (sahn-DEE-ah): Watermelon.

sangria (sahn-GREE-ah): A drink made of wine, fruit juice, and marinated fruits.

sangrita (sahn-GREE-tah): A drink made of orange and lime juice, grenadine, and Tabasco.

serape (sah-RAH-peh): A colorful woolen shawl worn over the shoulders.

serrano (seh-RRAH-noh): A type of small, fresh green chile.

sopa (SOH-pah): Soup.

sopa de lima (SOH-pah deh LEE-mah): Lime soup.

sopa seca (SOH-pah SEH-kah): Dry soup served as a side dish.

T

taceria (tah-keh-REE-ah): A taco stand.

taco (TAH-koh): A soft, corn tortilla with savory filling and garnish eaten like a sandwich.

tacos al carbon (TAH-kohs ahl kahr-BOHN): Grilled meat tacos.

tamale (tah-MAH-leh): Corn husk stuffed with corn dough and savory fillings and steamed.

tequila (teh-KEE-lah): A Mexican liquor distilled from the heart of the agave or maguey plant.

texate (teh-HAH-teh): The fruit of the mamey tree used to make a slightly sweet, milky drink.

Tikin-Chik (TIK-in-chik): A Yucatecan dish of marinated and grilled fish.

tomatillo (toh-mah-TEE-yoh): A small, green, acidic Mexican fruit used for salsas and marinades.

torta (TOHR-tah): A sandwich.

tortilla (tohr-TEE-yah): A round thin cake of unleavened, ground, dried corn eaten as bread in Mexico.

tostada (tohs-TAH-thah): A salad served on a fried corn tortilla.

v

vitriolla (bee-tree-OH-yah): A street vendor of cold juices and teas.

z

Zapotec (SAH-poh-tehk): Indian tribe of Oaxaca, Mexico.

zócalo (SOH-kah-loh): Mexican public square located in the center of town.